The Usborne
Science Experiments

Jane Bingham

Edited by Christopher Rawson

Designed by Susie McCaffre

Additional material by Rebecca Hed

CONTENTS

Illustrated by Peter Geissler and Joseph McEwan

Cover illustration by Kuo Kang Chen

Science Consultants: Julian Marshall,
Julie Deegan, Richard Hatton, Katherine Millett,
Sue North, Terry Allsop.

ABOUT EXPERIMENTING

Science can be intimidating, but when you try things out for yourself, ideas that seemed hard at first become much easier to understand.

This book will help you explore basic principles of physics, chemistry and biology by trying experiments on your own and with your friends.

How to use this book

The book is divided into over thirty scientific topics, such as "Floating and sinking", "Investigating acids" and "Making microbes work". You can try any experiment on its own, or work your way through a complete topic.

Clear explanations and diagrams show you exactly what is happening in the experiments and "Did you know?" boxes link your investigations to examples in the real world.

On pages 60-64, you can find more advanced scientific information, a list of science words with their definitions, and an index.

How to experiment

Scientists experiment to test their ideas. Before you start an experiment, try to predict what will happen and why. Then try the experiment. Read the explanation afterwards to see if you were right.

What you need

You don't need expensive apparatus to experiment. All the projects in this book use ordinary household objects or things you can buy from your local shops.

Following instructions

Scientists are always very careful and accurate. Follow the instructions exactly and always use clean equipment.

Getting it right

Don't worry if your experiment doesn't work at first. Try to think what could have gone wrong, adjust your equipment and try again.

This instrument, which shows changes in wind speed, is made from things you can easily find at home (see page 50).

If you use too much yeast in the experiment on page 32, you could get very messy.

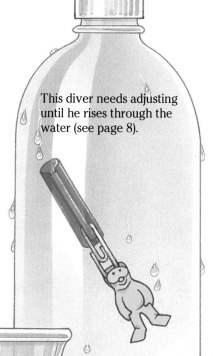

This diver needs adjusting until he rises through the water (see page 8).

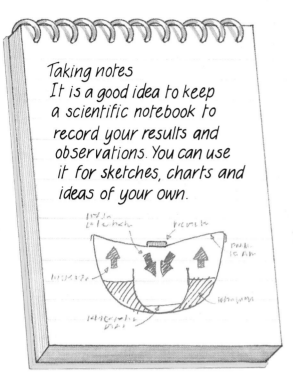

Taking notes
It is a good idea to keep a scientific notebook to record your results and observations. You can use it for sketches, charts and ideas of your own.

Safety first

All the experiments in this book are safe, as long as you follow the instructions carefully. Watch out for the symbols shown below. They warn you of possible dangers and remind you to take extra care.

 Experiments with electricity have this symbol. Never use household electricity for experiments. It is much too strong.

 This symbol warns you about chemicals. Wash your hands after handling chemicals and keep them away from young children.

 This is a general warning symbol. Be very careful whenever you see it, and take extra care with hot liquids, flames and sharp knives.

Watching results

Some results happen very slowly, but others are almost instant. If you missed what happened the first time, try the experiment again.

Why experiment?

Experimenting helps you discover more about the way things work and why things happen in the world around you.

The candle in a glass, on page 7, uses up its oxygen in a few seconds.

The garden in a jar, on page 46, takes a few weeks to grow.

Making and controlling this spider on a string (see page 31) will help you understand how your bicycle brakes work.

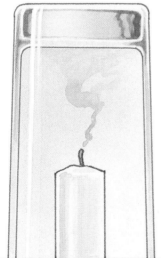

The experiment to make a wire sink through ice, on page 42, shows what happens when you go ice-skating.

BALANCING AND GRAVITY

If you drop a ruler, an invisible force called gravity pulls it to Earth. If you rest its mid-point on your finger, gravity pulls down equally on both sides of the ruler and it balances in the air. The experiments on these two pages show you some ways of using the force of gravity to make things balance, stay upright or fall over.

Make a mobile

Mobiles balance perfectly when gravity pulls equally on every part of them. Follow the steps below to make a mobile from garden cane, thread, and cardboard covered with foil. Then experiment with each part of your mobile to find the point where it balances best. This is called its centre of gravity.

1 Use a sharp knife to cut some thin garden cane into one 30cm (12in) length and three 15cm (6in) lengths.

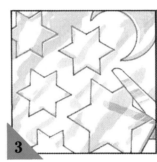

2 Cut the side off an empty cereal packet, then use paper glue to stick aluminium foil* onto both sides of it.

3 Draw five equal-sized stars, one big star and a moon on the foil-covered card. Then cut out the shapes.

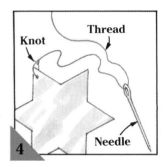

4 Use a needle to thread long pieces of thread through the tops of all the shapes. Then knot them securely.

Balancing the mobile

Knot or tape the stars on threads to the three short rods. Then balance each rod by hanging it from a loosely knotted thread and sliding the rod sideways until it hangs level. Secure the thread with a thin strip of sticky tape** or a knot.

Hang the three short rods from the long rod. One side of the long rod will point up in the air. Tie the moon shape onto that side, then slide it sideways until the mobile is perfectly balanced.

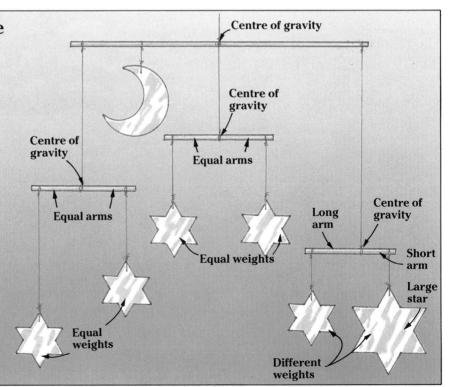

4   ***Aluminum foil (US).***   *** Cellophane tape (US).***

Make a clown that won't lie down

All objects have a centre of gravity, where the object balances and all its weight seems to be concentrated. Top-heavy objects have a high centre of gravity, which makes them easy to tip over. Objects with heavy bases have a low centre of gravity, which makes them more stable. Follow the instructions below to make this clown. Then try changing its centre of gravity and watch the effect that gravity has on it.

You will need
Ping-pong ball
Thick paper 10cm x 5cm
  (4in x 2in)
Scissors
Sticky tape
Pen
Plasticine *

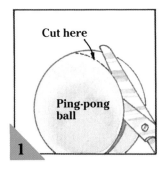

1 Push one blade of your scissors into the ping-pong ball on the join line. Cut all the way around the line.

2 Roll the paper so that it fits snugly inside one half of the ball. Then tape up the side of the paper to make a tube.

3 Tape the bottom of the paper tube to the ball. Draw a face on the paper, supporting it from the back with two fingers.

4 Your clown will not stand up. Press plasticine into the clown's base to make it stand. Then try to push it over.

Why the clown won't lie down

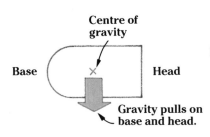

Centre of gravity
Base — Head
Gravity pulls on base and head.

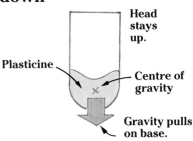

Head stays up.
Plasticine — Centre of gravity
Gravity pulls on base.

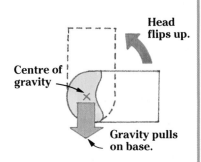

Head flips up.
Centre of gravity
Gravity pulls on base.

Without plasticine in its base, the clown's centre of gravity is around its middle. Gravity pulls equally on the clown's head and on its base, so it stays down.

When you push in the plasticine, the clown has a new centre of gravity in its base. Now gravity pulls on the clown's base, so it stands up.

When you try to tip over the weighted clown, gravity still pulls on its base, but not on its head, so the base stays down and the head flips up.

Now try this

Take the plasticine lump out of the ping-pong ball and drop in a marble. Now tape the other half of the ball to the open end of the paper tube.

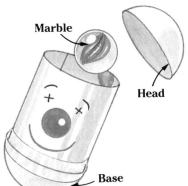

Marble
Head
Base

Stand your clown on a gentle slope. It will flip from head to base and over again as the rolling marble makes the centre of gravity move from one end of the clown to the other.

* Plastic modelling clay (US). 5

IT'S A GAS

The air around you is made up of different gases. When you breathe in, you absorb oxygen from the air. This is the gas that keeps you alive. When you breathe out, you send a waste gas called carbon dioxide into the air. Try the experiments on these two pages to find out more about oxygen and carbon dioxide.

Make carbon dioxide gas

Your body produces carbon dioxide gas as a waste product, but it can be made in other ways. Look in your kitchen cupboards for vinegar and bicarbonate of soda, or buy them at a supermarket. Then make the apparatus shown in the picture below.

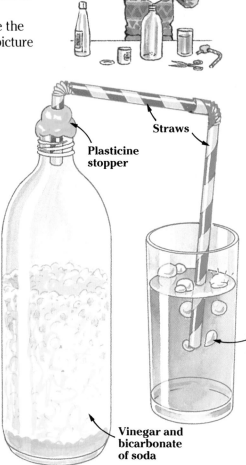

You will need

Plasticine
2 bendy drinking straws
Scissors
Tall glass
Food colouring
Bicarbonate of soda
Vinegar
Plastic bottle
Small piece of paper

1 Roll a strip of plasticine around the short end of a bendy straw, taking care not to crush the straw.

2 Cut a slit in the other end of the straw and slide it inside the second straw, so it fits tightly.

3 Fill the glass with water. Then stir in a drop of food colouring.

Straws

Plasticine stopper

Bubbles of carbon dioxide gas

Vinegar and bicarbonate of soda

4 Pour half a tablespoon of bicarbonate of soda down a folded piece of paper into the glass bottle, as shown in the picture above. Then pour in vinegar until the bottle is a quarter full.

5 Quickly push the plasticine around the top of the bottle and put the end of the second straw in the glass of coloured water. Watch what happens in the water.

How you make the gas

When you mix an acid like vinegar (ethanoic acid) with a carbonate like bicarbonate of soda, they react and make carbon dioxide gas. The gas builds up and is pushed along the straw into the water. Carbon dioxide gas is less dense than water so it bubbles to the surface.

Using oxygen

Flames need oxygen to burn just like human beings need oxygen to breathe. Here is an experiment that uses a burning candle in a glass to show how much oxygen there is in the air.

⚠ Be very careful with lighted matches and candles.

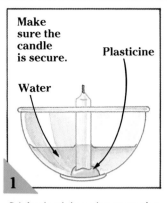

Make sure the candle is secure.
Plasticine
Water

1 Stick plasticine pieces on the base of a candle and on opposite sides of the rim of a tall glass. Stand the candle in a bowl and pour in water, as shown here.

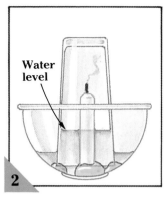

Water level

2 Light the candle. Allow it to burn for a few seconds, then stand the glass over it. What happens to the candle? Where is the water level in the glass?

What happens to the oxygen

The candle burns until it has used up all the oxygen in the glass. As oxygen is used, water takes its place. The water rises about one-fifth of the way up the glass because oxygen makes up around one-fifth of the gases in air.

Make a fire extinguisher

Many extinguishers contain compressed carbon dioxide which puts out fires by preventing oxygen from reaching the flames. Here is an experiment to make carbon dioxide gas and test it on a night-light candle.

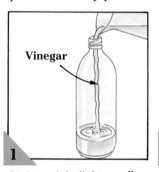

Vinegar

1 Light a night-light candle. Then pour five tablespoons of vinegar (ethanoic acid) into a small glass bottle.

Bicarbonate of soda

2 Pour half a tablespoon of bicarbonate of soda down a folded piece of paper into the bottle. The mixture should fizz.

3 Hold the bottle sideways over the night-light, making sure no liquid escapes. What happens to the flame?

Why the flame goes out

The acid and the carbonate react to make carbon dioxide gas, which is heavier than oxygen. The oxygen is pushed away, so the candle cannot burn.

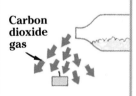

Carbon dioxide gas

Did you know?

Plants and trees help to keep the balance of oxygen and carbon dioxide gases in the air. At night, they take in oxygen and send out carbon dioxide, like other living things. In sunlight, they use carbon dioxide to make food and oxygen.

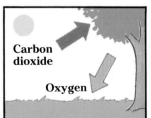

Carbon dioxide
Oxygen

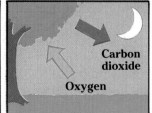

Carbon dioxide
Oxygen

FLOATING AND SINKING

Have you noticed that some things, like stones, always sink, but others, like cork, always float? This is not because they are heavy or light − even light stones sink − but because they are heavy or light for their size. The heaviness of an object for its size is called its density. Try the experiments on these two pages to find out more about density.

Cork is light for its size, so it floats.

Stones are heavy for their size, so they sink.

Sink the orange

Float an orange in a bowl of water and challenge a friend to make it sink. Now peel the orange. Put it back in the water and watch what happens.

Why the orange sinks

Orange peel is full of trapped air bubbles. This makes the orange light for its size, so it floats. Without its peel and the air bubbles inside it, the orange weighs a lot for its size. The peeled orange is more dense than water, so it sinks.

Diver in a bottle

Follow the instructions to make this model diver. Then make it float and sink by changing its density.

Squeeze the bottle to make the diver sink.

Relax your grip to make the diver rise.

You will need

Plastic pen top with clip
Plasticine
Paper-clip
Large plastic bottle with screw cap

Figure must fit through neck of bottle.

1 Make a plasticine figure 3.5cm (1.25in) long. Fix the paper-clip to its head and hang it from the pen top. Fill the bottle with water and drop in the diver.

Pour in water until it overflows.

2 The pen top should float with its top just above the water level. Make the figure bigger or smaller if needed. Then pour in more water and screw the cap on tightly.

Why the diver rises and sinks

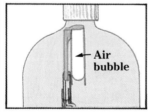

Air bubble

When you put the pen top in the water, a bubble of air is trapped inside it. This trapped air bubble makes the diver less dense than water, so it floats.

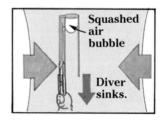

Squashed air bubble

Diver sinks.

When you squeeze the bottle, water squashes the air* and takes up more space in the pen top. Now the diver is more dense than water, so it sinks.

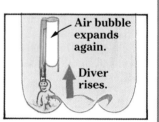

Air bubble expands again.

Diver rises.

When you relax your grip on the bottle, the air in the pen top expands again. Now the diver is less dense than water, so it comes back up to the surface.

8

*For more about squashing air, see page 34.

Raise the raisins

All you need for this experiment is a jar full of clear fizzy drink* and a handful of raisins to drop into the drink. It works because the bubbles of carbon dioxide gas in the drink are much less dense than the drink or the raisins. Once the raisins have started to move, they will keep rising and falling inside the jar for about an hour.

1. The raisins are more dense than the drink, so they sink.

2. Gas bubbles stick to the wrinkles on the raisins.

4. Gas bubbles burst. Now the raisins are more dense than the drink, so they sink again.

3. Raisins covered with bubbles are less dense than the drink, so they rise.

Float the egg

In the last three experiments, you changed the density of different objects to make them float or sink. Here is a way to make an egg float, by changing the density of the water, not the egg.

1
Gently lower an egg into a large glass of water. It will sink because it is more dense than water. Rescue the egg.

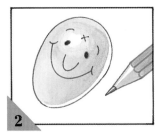

Cloudy brine will clear.

2
Pour ten tablespoons of salt into the water, and stir until it all dissolves. This salt and water solution is called brine.

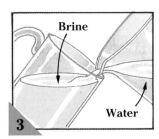

3
Put the egg in the brine. Now it should float, because the salt has made the water more dense than the egg.

Suspend the egg

Once you know how to make an egg float, you can amaze your friends by suspending the egg in the middle of a glass. For a really spooky effect, draw a face on it first.

Hold egg in place when marking it.

1
Float the egg in the brine and make a pencil mark on its highest point. Take the egg out of the brine and dry it.

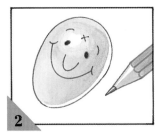

2
Draw a face on the egg, with the pencil mark between its eyebrows. Draw another face on the opposite side.

Brine

Water

3
Pour away brine until the glass is half full. Tilt the glass gently, then slowly pour cold water on top of the brine.

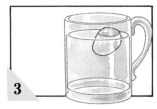

4
When the glass is full, carefully slide in the egg. It should sink through the water and float on the brine.

How the egg stays there

The water and the egg are less dense than the brine so they float on top of it. You can show how water floats on brine by doing the same experiment with some food colouring in the water.

SOUNDS INTERESTING

Have you ever wondered how you hear things? On these two pages, you can investigate how sounds reach your ears and find out more about how sound travels. You can also experiment with making high and low sounds.

Feel the vibrations

Did you know that sounds make vibrations that you can feel? This test will help you understand how your ears work.

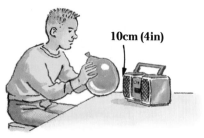

10cm (4in)

Turn on a radio. Then hold a balloon about 10cm (4in) away from it. What do you feel? Turn up the volume on the radio and hold the balloon again. What do you feel now?

How your ear feels vibrations

All sounds make the air vibrate. When sound vibrations hit your eardrum, which is a thin sheet of skin, it starts vibrating too, like the balloon.

Vibrations from your eardrum become louder in your middle ear and are changed into electrical messages in your inner ear.

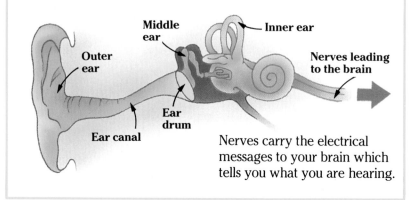

Middle ear
Inner ear
Outer ear
Nerves leading to the brain
Ear drum
Ear canal

Nerves carry the electrical messages to your brain which tells you what you are hearing.

Watch sound travel

This experiment with a drum made from a plastic bottle shows that sound vibrations travel through the air. You also need a plastic bag, an elastic band, scissors and a night-light candle.

Plastic bottle

1

Cut the base off the bottle. Then cut a piece from the plastic bag to cover the end of the bottle.

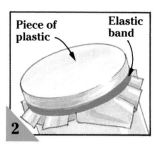

Piece of plastic
Elastic band

2

Stretch the piece of plastic tightly over the end of the bottle. Secure it with an elastic band.

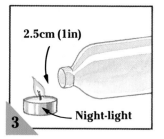

2.5cm (1in)

Night-light

3

Light a night-light candle. Then hold the bottle about 2.5cm (1in) away from the candle.

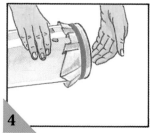

4

Tap the piece of plastic sharply with your fingertips. What happens to the flame?

How sound travels

When you tap the piece of plastic you make tiny particles in the air beside it vibrate. These vibrating particles make the particles beside them vibrate, too. The vibrations travel through the bottle and blow out the flame.

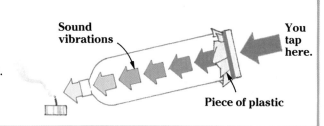

Sound vibrations
You tap here.
Piece of plastic

Sound through a tube

For this sound test you need a long tube, made from cardboard or rolled-up paper, and a watch that ticks.

1 Hold the watch by your ear and move it away until you cannot hear it ticking any more. How far do you have to move it?

2 Cover the watch with the tube and hold the other end of the tube against your ear. Now can you hear anything?

How the tube works

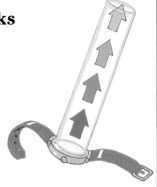

Sound vibrations need energy to travel. As they spread out, they lose energy. That is why you stop hearing the watch tick.

When sound vibrations are trapped in the tube they do not lose so much energy. So you hear the watch tick through the tube.

Changing sound

Here is a simple way to change the sound vibrations inside a plastic drinking straw.

Blow steadily across the top of the straw while a friend cuts pieces off it. Do this very carefully. How does the sound change?

Why the sound changes

When you blow across the top of the straw, air vibrates inside it and makes a sound. As the straw gets shorter, the air loses less energy and vibrates faster, making a higher sound.

Now try this

Tape plastic straws of different lengths to a cardboard strip. Blow across the ends of the straws to make high and low notes.

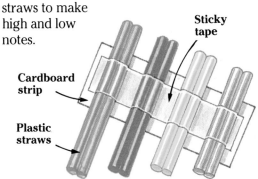

Sticky tape

Cardboard strip

Plastic straws

Bottle sounds

Find two identical glass bottles and fill them with different amounts of water. Then try making high and low sounds, like this.

1 Blow across the top of each of the bottles. Which one makes the higher note?

2 Tap each of the bottles with a spoon. Which bottle makes the higher note now?

How you make bottle sounds

When you blow across the top of the bottles, the air inside them vibrates. When you tap them with a spoon, the water vibrates.

Small amounts of air or water vibrate fast and make a high sound. Larger amounts vibrate more slowly and make a low sound.

Blow for a high note.

Tap for a low note.

Blow for a low note.

Tap for a high note.

SURPRISING SENSES

You use your senses all the time, but have you ever thought what happens when you hear, see, touch, taste or smell things? Each of these experiments concentrates on a different sense to help you find out more about the way your body works.

Where's the sound?

Have you ever wondered why you have two ears? Try this test with a jar half-full of dried beans, a blindfold and a friend.

1 Sit on a chair and blindfold yourself. Then ask your friend to rattle the jar in different places around your head.

2 Point to where you think the sounds come from. How many did you get right?

Rattle the jar in lots of places.

Why you need two ears

You need two ears so your brain can compare noise levels reaching each ear and work out exactly where a sound comes from. When a sound comes from a point that is equally distant from both your ears, it is hard to judge where that point is.

Jar

One eye teaser

You use both your eyes, like you use both your ears, to work out exactly where things are. This experiment shows you why two eyes give you better vision than one.

Close one eye, then hold up a pen in one hand and its top in the other, so they are level with your eyes. With your arms slightly bent, try to put the top on the pen. Can you tell if the top is in front or behind the pen? Now try again using both eyes and see if it is easier.

Keep one eye tightly shut.

Why you need two eyes

Pen   **Top**

Two eyes give you two slightly different views. Your brain compares these two views to work out exactly where things are.

When you close one eye, you have only one view, so it is much harder for your brain to judge the distance between objects.

Did you know?

Animals that pounce on their prey, such as owls and cats, have forward-facing eyes, like human beings, which help them judge distances accurately. The animals they prey on, such as mice and rabbits, have eyes in the sides of their heads. This gives them better all-round vision.

Touch test

Whenever you touch something, tiny nerve endings near the surface of your skin send messages to your brain. In places where you are sensitive, these nerve endings are close together. In other places, they are wider apart. Try this test with a friend, a blindfold and two sharp pencils to find where you are most sensitive.

Make a tongue map

Did you know you use different parts of your tongue to taste things that are sour, salty, sweet and bitter? Draw a map of your tongue like the one here. Then try the tests below and fill in your results.* (Some tastes are detected in more than one place.)

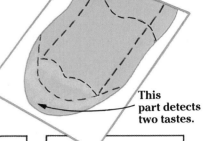

This part detects two tastes.

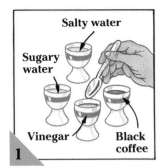

Salty water

Sugary water

Vinegar

Black coffee

1

Fill four egg-cups with different tasting liquids: vinegar (sour); salty water (salt); sugary water (sweet); and black coffee (bitter).

Drinking straw dropper

Vinegar

2

Cut two straws in half to make droppers. Dip a dropper into the vinegar. Cover the end with your finger to hold in some liquid.

Release finger.

Squeeze here.

Drop of liquid

3

Carefully release drops of liquid onto each area of your tongue shown on the map, drying your tongue with bread between drops.

4

Note on your map where you taste the vinegar most strongly. Rinse your mouth, then do the same test for the three other tastes.

No nose surprise

In this experiment, you stop your sense of smell from working so you can see how it affects the way you taste things.

Grate raw apple, carrot and potato into three bowls. Then blindfold yourself and hold your nose. Ask a friend to feed you a spoonful of each food, one at a time. Can you recognize which food you are tasting?

Hold your nose very tightly.

Carrot — Apple — Potato

How your nose helps you taste

Tiny particles of food in the air and in your mouth travel into your nose, so you taste and smell together. Your tongue tells you that apple, potato and carrot taste sweet, but you need your nose to recognize their flavours.

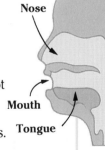

Nose

Mouth

Tongue

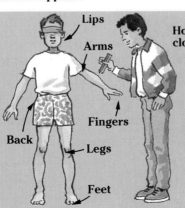

Lips

Arms

Hold the two pencils close together.

Fingers

Back

Legs

Feet

1 Blindfold yourself. Then ask a friend to touch you very lightly in all the places labelled in the picture, using sometimes one pencil and sometimes two.

2 Say when you feel two points and when you feel only one. You will be right most often in the places where your nerve endings are closer together.

Did you know?

Flies use their feet to taste their food. Before they eat anything, they walk all over it.

* *Check your results on page 60.*

LIGHT AND SIGHT

Light travels through the air in straight lines. If it did not, there would be no shadows and you would not be able to see. Try these experiments in the dark to discover more about how shadows are made and how your eyes use light to see things.

Shadow portrait

1 At night-time, ask a friend to stand by a closed door. Then use masking tape to stick a large piece of paper behind his head.

2 Turn off the light and shine a torch* at your friend's head. What do you see?

3 Slowly move your torch closer to his head. What happens to the shadow now?

4 When you have made a giant shadow that you like, ask another friend to draw around it on the piece of paper.

How shadows are made

When rays of light meet an object, they bounce or reflect off it. A shadow is made behind the object where no light gets through. As you move your torch closer, more light is blocked and the shadow gets bigger.

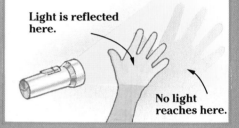

Light is reflected here.

No light reaches here.

Spooky shadow

When light rays meet a smooth, shiny surface, like a mirror, they bounce off the mirror like a ball off a wall, and you see a reflection.** This experiment combines shadows with reflections.

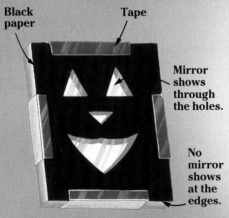

Black paper

Tape

Mirror shows through the holes.

No mirror shows at the edges.

You will need
Black paper
Scissors
Sticky tape
Mirror
Table lamp
   without a shade

1 Cut out a piece of black paper to fit over the mirror. Draw a face on the paper and cut it out. Tape the paper over the mirror.

2 Put the lamp on the floor and turn it on. Ask a friend to stand in front of the lamp so she casts a shadow on the wall.

3 Hold the mirror behind the lamp. Move it around until the cut-out shapes are reflected onto the shadow on the wall.

Flashlight (US).   ** *See pages 16-17 for more about reflections.*

Make a yogurt pot viewer

Because light travels in straight lines, something strange happens when light rays from an object pass through a small hole and land on a screen. Follow the instructions below to make this simple viewer. Then point it at a night-light in a dark room and look at its screen.

You will need
Yogurt pot
Black poster paint
Dishwashing liquid
Drawing-pin *
Elastic band
Greaseproof paper **
Night-light candle
Ruler

Black paint reduces reflections inside pot.

1

Paint the inside of the yogurt pot with black poster paint. If you mix a drop of dishwashing liquid with the paint, it will stick better.

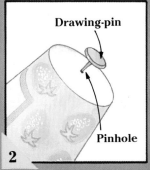

Drawing-pin

Pinhole

2

When the paint is dry, make a pinhole in the base of the yogurt pot with the drawing-pin. Then ease the pin out carefully.

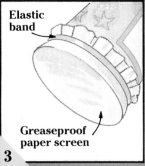

Elastic band

Greaseproof paper screen

3

Stretch a piece of greaseproof paper tightly over the top of the pot and secure it with an elastic band. This is your viewer's screen.

Hold the viewer level with your eyes.

Screen

4

Light the candle, make the room dark and point the viewer's base at the candle, from about 50cm (20in) away. What do you see on the screen?

How the viewer works

Some light from the flame travels through the pinhole and lands on the paper screen. Light rays from the top of the flame hit the bottom part of the screen and rays from the bottom hit the top part of the screen, making an upside-down image.

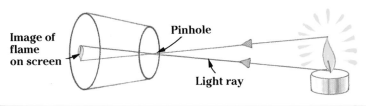

Image of flame on screen

Pinhole

Light ray

Light from flame

Now try this

Take your viewer outside on a sunny day. Cover your head with a coat so only the viewer's base is exposed. What do you see on the screen?

Did you know?

Your eyes work like the yogurt pot viewer. Light travels through a tiny hole called a pupil and lands on a screen called a retina, making an upside-down image. The optic nerve joins your retina to your brain which turns the image the right way up and tells you what you are seeing.

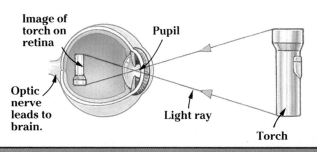

Image of torch on retina

Pupil

Optic nerve leads to brain.

Light ray

Torch

* Push-pin (US).   *** Waxed paper (US).*

BOUNCING LIGHT

When light meets a shiny surface like a mirror, it bounces off it and is reflected back. The experiments on these two pages will help you understand more about reflected light and mirrors. You can also use reflections to create some strange effects.

Bouncing spotlight

Can you predict how a light beam will reflect off a mirror? Try this test with a torch, a book and a watch, arranged as shown in the picture below.

1 Darken the room and point your torch at the mirror. Keep changing the angle of the torch until the reflected light beam lights up the watch's face.

2 Now move the watch sideways. Can you aim the torch so the watch lights up first time? Try it with the watch in several different positions.

How light bounces

Light always bounces off a mirror in the same way. Whatever the angle at which it hits the mirror, it will be reflected at the same angle.

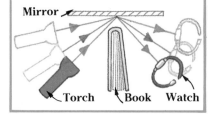

Using reflections

Once you can predict how light will be reflected, you can use mirrors to help you see things. The picture below shows some ways of using reflected light to see from awkward positions.

Look over things.

Look around things.

Look under things.

Mirror drawing

Draw a simple shape and stand a mirror behind it. Look in the mirror and try to draw over your shape.

What you draw

When you look in the mirror, the top of your picture becomes the bottom. This makes it very difficult to draw around, especially when the lines change direction.

Message in a can

You have probably tried "mirror writing" with a flat mirror, but have you ever used a shiny can to send a secret message?

Stand the can on a piece of paper. Then write a message so it looks correct in the can. The letters on the paper will be upside-down and reversed. Your friends will be able to read your message in a can of the same size.

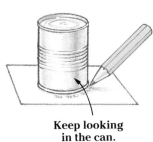

Keep looking in the can.

Candle illusion

Here is a way to create a dramatic effect, using a perspex picture frame* as a window and as a mirror at the same time. This experiment also shows that an object and its reflection are always the same distance from a mirror.

1 Stand the frame between the night-light candles. Ask a friend to light one. Then move the other until your friend sees a reflected flame on its wick.

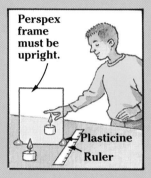

Perspex frame must be upright.

Plasticine
Ruler

2 Now put your finger on the wick of the unlit candle. Your friend will think your finger is burning.

3 Measure the distances between each candle and the frame. They should be exactly the same.

Why it works

Your friend sees the unlit candle and your finger through the frame. At the same time, light from the lighted candle is reflected by the frame. So your finger appears to be in the flame.

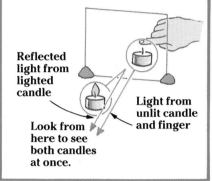

Reflected light from lighted candle

Light from unlit candle and finger

Look from here to see both candles at once.

Pepper's ghost

The trick of reflection shown above can be used on stage to make ghosts appear to walk through walls. You can create the same effect in a peep-hole theatre made from a shoe box.

1 Tape the postcard to the back of the box, then cut a slit in the box beneath the postcard.

2 Use a ball-point pen to make a peep-hole in the shoe box, facing the card.

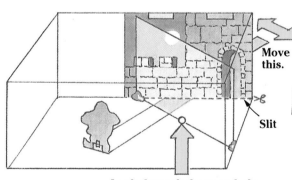

Move this.

Slit

Look through the peep-hole.

3 Make a ghost from stiff white paper like the one shown below. Tape the cardboard strip to the ghost's back and then bend the strip upwards. Slide the end of the strip through the slit at the back of the box.

4 Secure the perspex frame with plasticine so it stands diagonally in front of the peep-hole. Now the ghost faces the frame, but cannot be seen from the peep-hole.

How the ghost appears

When you look through the peep-hole, you see the scenery through the frame and the ghost reflected by the frame.

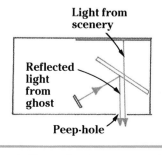

Light from scenery

Reflected light from ghost

Peep-hole

Copy this same size.

You see this.

* Clear plastic picture frame (US).

BENDING LIGHT

You see things when light is reflected from them and travels straight through the air to your eyes. Things look strange underwater, because light travels from them in a different way. These experiments show you how light travels through water.

Watch light bend

Here is a way to see what happens when a beam of light travels from the air into water and then back into the air again. Do it in the dark, so you can see the light beam clearly.

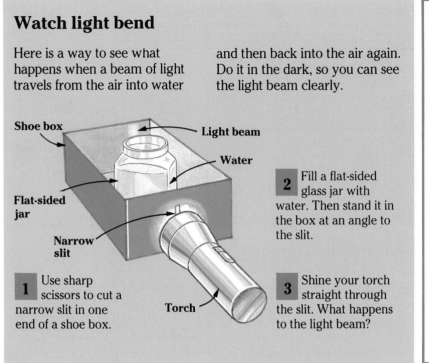

Shoe box — Light beam
Water
Flat-sided jar
Narrow slit
Torch

1 Use sharp scissors to cut a narrow slit in one end of a shoe box.

2 Fill a flat-sided glass jar with water. Then stand it in the box at an angle to the slit.

3 Shine your torch straight through the slit. What happens to the light beam?

Why light bends

Light moves more slowly through water than it moves through air. As the beam of light enters the water, it slows down and bends. As it re-enters the air, the light beam speeds up and bends back again. This is called refraction.

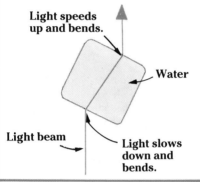

Light speeds up and bends.
Water
Light beam
Light slows down and bends.

Rising coin

Have you noticed that things at the bottom of a pool or river always look closer to the surface than they really are? This is an effect of refracted light. To see it for yourself, try this experiment with a friend.

Coin is out of sight.

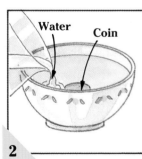

Water
Coin

1 Put a coin in a china or plastic bowl. Then walk backwards until you cannot see the coin in the bowl any more.

2 Ask a friend to pour water slowly into the bowl. Watch the bowl from where you are standing. What do you see?

Why the coin seems to rise

At first, you see the coin inside the bowl, because light travels straight from the coin to your eyes. When you move away, light from the coin no longer reaches your eyes, so you only see the bowl.

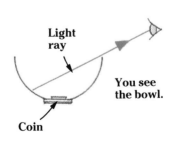

Light ray
You see the bowl.
Coin

As the bowl fills with water, light from the coin is refracted by the water. Now light from the coin reaches your eyes again, so you see the coin in the bowl.

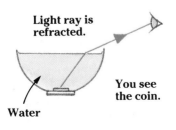

Light ray is refracted.
You see the coin.
Water

STARTING AND STOPPING

It is hard to get things moving, especially if they are heavy, and once they are moving it is hard to make them stop. Things stay still or keep moving because of something called inertia. All the experiments on this page investigate inertia.

Orange drop

Lay a postcard on a mug. Stand a matchbox cover in the middle of the card and balance an orange on top of it. Now pull the card away quickly. What happens to the orange?

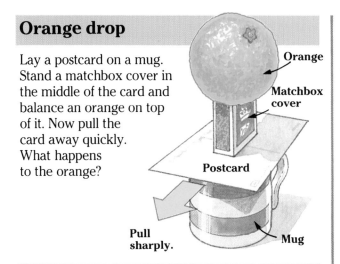

Orange

Matchbox cover

Postcard

Pull sharply.

Mug

Why the orange drops

Heavy things, like the orange, have more inertia than light things, like the card and the matchbox cover. Inertia stops the orange from getting going, so it drops into the mug.

Coin challenge

This experiment works, like the one on the left, because heavy objects have greater inertia than light objects.

1 Thick coins work best.

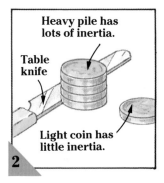

Heavy pile has lots of inertia.

Table knife

Light coin has little inertia.

2

Make a pile of five identical coins, then challenge your friends to remove the bottom coin without touching the rest of the pile.

Knock the bottom coin with the edge of a table knife. It will slide sideways, but inertia will prevent the other coins from moving with it.

Stop the egg

Inertia makes things difficult to stop, as well as hard to get started. Try this experiment with an uncooked egg.

1 Set the egg spinning on a plate. Then touch it lightly with your finger to stop it.

2 As soon as the egg stops, take your finger away. What happens to the egg?

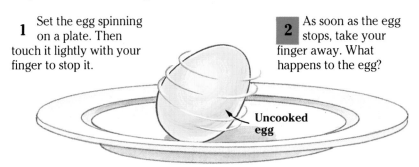

Uncooked egg

Why the egg won't stop

When you put your finger on the egg, you stop the shell, but inertia keeps the white and the yolk spinning. When you let go, the moving contents make the egg start spinning again. A hard-boiled egg would not start again because its contents are solid.

Wearing seatbelts

When a car crashes, it is forced to stop suddenly, but its passengers must be made to stop, too. If the passengers are not wearing seatbelts, their inertia will keep them moving forwards and they could go through the windscreen.*

Car manufacturers use plastic dummies, like the one shown here, to test their seatbelts.

TURN AND TURN AGAIN

Things which are moving always travel in straight lines, unless something forces them to change direction. The experiments on these two pages will help you understand some of the strange effects of forcing things to turn.

Turn the corner

Have you ever been pushed against the side door, when the car in which you are travelling turns a corner sharply? Try this test, using a light coin as the passenger and a tray as the car, to see why this happens.

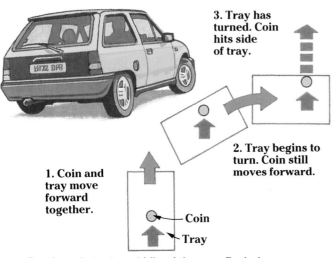

3. Tray has turned. Coin hits side of tray.

2. Tray begins to turn. Coin still moves forward.

1. Coin and tray move forward together.

Coin

Tray

Put the coin in the middle of the tray. Push the tray forwards, then turn it sharply to the right. The coin should keep travelling forwards until it hits the side of the tray. Like the coin, the passenger in the car continues travelling forwards as the car turns, until he is pushed against its side.

Swing the bucket

This surprising experiment works in the same way as the one with the coin on a tray, but instead of making the bucket turn a corner once, you keep on turning it around.

1 Half fill a plastic bucket with water. Stand outside and swing it in a circle.

2 If you make the bucket swing fast enough, no water will spill out of it.

Bucket turns this way.

Water tries to travel this way.

What happens in the bucket

When you swing the bucket, you keep forcing it to change direction, but the water inside the bucket still tries to travel in straight lines. The water is pushed against the inside of the bucket and cannot fall out.

Raise the ball

1 Make a plasticine ball about the size of a marble. Put it on a table and stand a jar with a neck over it.

2 Challenge a friend to lift the ball off the table without touching the ball or tipping the jar.

3 Twist the jar sharply to set the ball spinning. Lift the jar. The spinning ball will be lifted up inside it.

Why the ball rises

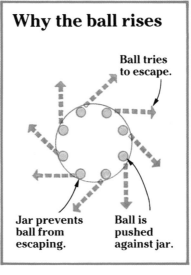

Ball tries to escape.

Jar prevents ball from escaping.

Ball is pushed against jar.

Did you know?

Bobsleighs are pushed against the curved walls of their track just like the ball is pushed against the inside of the jar in the experiment on the left.

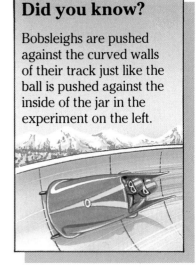

Draw a circle from straight lines

Here is a good way to understand what is happening in the other experiments on these two pages. The straight lines show the direction that a spinning object would take, if it were not being forced to turn. The circle shows the direction that the spinning object is forced to take.

1 Cut the side panel off a cereal packet, making sure that its edges are straight. This is your ruler.

2 Stick a drawing-pin through the middle of the ruler and pin it to a sheet of paper, on top of a magazine.

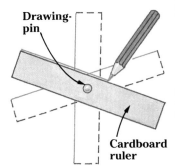

Drawing-pin

Cardboard ruler

3 Draw a line along the top of the ruler. Now turn the ruler slightly and rule another line along the top.

4 Keep turning the ruler and ruling lines, until you have drawn a complete circle from straight lines.

Lift the pot

Can you make a hard sweet* lift a pot of stones? This experiment shows you how to do it.

You will need

Empty pen case
Ball-point pen
Table knife
Hard sweet
Yogurt pot
String, Stones

1 Make two holes in the sides of the yogurt pot with a ball-point pen. Make a handle by threading a short string through the holes. Tie a 40cm (16in) string to the handle and thread it through the pen case.

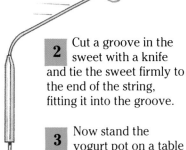

2 Cut a groove in the sweet with a knife and tie the sweet firmly to the end of the string, fitting it into the groove.

3 Now stand the yogurt pot on a table and twist the pen case to set the sweet spinning. Gently raise the pen case. When the sweet is spinning fast enough, it will lift the pot of stones off the table.

Why the pot lifts

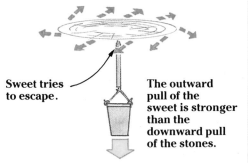

Sweet tries to escape.

The outward pull of the sweet is stronger than the downward pull of the stones.

The spinning sweet tries to travel away from the end of the pen case, but the weight of the stones holds it back, so it moves in a circle. The more you twist the pen case, the faster the sweet spins around. When the pull of the sweet is stronger than the downward pull of the stones, the sweet lifts the pot.

Did you know?

Satellites circle the Earth because the Earth's gravity pulls on them and makes them turn, just like the pot of stones pulled on the sweet. Because there is no connecting string between a satellite and the Earth, it has to travel at a precise speed to keep moving in a circle.

If the satellite travels too fast, it shoots into space.

If it goes too slowly, gravity pulls it to Earth.

Earth

* Hard candy (US).

FOLLOW THE FOOD TRAIL

These observations will help you find out more about the things small animals eat and the ways they search for their food.

⚠️ Treat the ants, worms and woodlice that you are watching very carefully.
Put them back where you found them after you have finished studying them.

Follow an ant trail

Ants are social insects that live together in nests. When an ant finds some food, it makes a trail for others to follow. Put a small piece of apple on a sheet of paper and lay the paper close to an ants' nest. Then watch the ants carefully.

1 Wait for some ants to find the apple. They should all take the same path.

Apple

Ant trail

2 Now move the apple. Do the ants go straight to it?

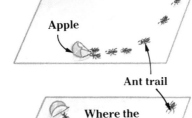

Antennae

Where the apple was.

How ants follow the trail

Once an ant has found some food, it produces special chemicals that leave a scent trail. Other ants from the nest use their antennae, or feelers, to sense this scent. Even after the food has moved, the ants still follow the old trail until a new one is laid.

Now try this

Rub out an ant trail by sprinkling it with soil. The ants should scurry around until they find the food and make a new trail.

Where to find ants, worms and woodlice

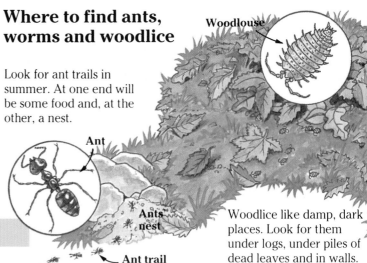

Woodlouse

Look for ant trails in summer. At one end will be some food and, at the other, a nest.

Ant

Ants' nest

Ant trail

Woodlice like damp, dark places. Look for them under logs, under piles of dead leaves and in walls.

Watching woodlice

Woodlice have sensitive antennae that help them to find food, even when they cannot see it. Make this T-junction in a box, then collect about six woodlice in a container with a lid. Gently release them into the box and watch how they use their antennae.

1 Cut the front panel off the cereal packet. Then cut the panel into three long strips.

Cardboard strips – don't leave gaps at the bottom.

Tape down lid.

Passage should be just wide enough for woodlice.

Leaves

Woodlice start here.

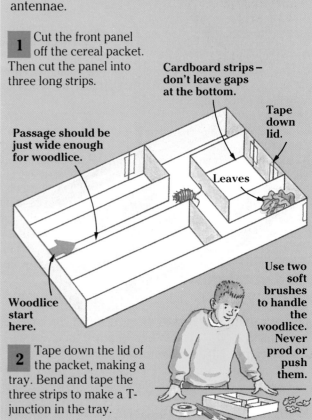

Use two soft brushes to handle the woodlice. Never prod or push them.

2 Tape down the lid of the packet, making a tray. Bend and tape the three strips to make a T-junction in the tray.

Never pull on worms. They are covered with bristles that grip the soil tightly.

Worm

Worms live under stones, in freshly dug soil, or near compost heaps. They come to the surface at night.

Make a wormery

Worms are hard to study because they are sensitive to light. To see how they live and feed, make a special home, like the one shown below. Then find two or three worms to put in it.

Handle the worms gently.

You will need

Shoe box
Sticky tape
Ball-point pen
Large plastic bottle
Scissors
3 mugs of damp, crumbly soil
1 mug of sand
Dry leaves
Small cubes of onion and potato

1 Tape the lid onto one side of the shoe box so it opens like a door. Pierce holes in the top of the box with a ball-point pen, to let air into the wormery.

2 Cut the top off the bottle. Then fill it with loosely packed layers of soil and sand, as shown here. Scatter the food on the surface.

3 Gently drop in your worms and stand the wormery in its box with the door closed. Leave it outside in a cool, dry place for four days.

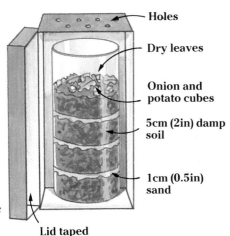

Holes

Dry leaves

Onion and potato cubes

5cm (2in) damp soil

1cm (0.5in) sand

Lid taped to box

You will need

Scissors
Dead, damp leaves
Sticky tape
2 soft paintbrushes
Mini cereal packet or small cardboard box

3 Let your woodlice walk along the passage, one at a time. When they reach the junction, some will turn left and some will turn right.

4 Now put some damp leaves in the right hand side of the box and let the woodlice walk through the box again. This time, their antennae should guide them towards the food.

Did you know?

Woodlice are crustaceans, which means they have a hard shell and are related to crabs and lobsters.

What happens in the wormery

The worms mix up the soil by coming to the surface for food and then tunnelling underground. Worms usually feed on decaying plant leaves and stems, so they should eat all the food in your wormery.

4 days later

Soil and sand are mixed.

Now put the worms back where you found them.

Did you know?

Worms are useful in gardens because they mix up the soil and let in air. They also make the soil richer by pulling food down into their tunnels.

23

INVESTIGATING ACIDS

Acids are chemicals that occur naturally in lots of different substances, including food and drinks. Did you know, for example, that cola, cheese and tea all contain acid?

On the next four pages you can discover more about acids and the way they react with other substances. You can also try a colourful acid test.

Adding acid

Food and drinks which contain a lot of acid have a sour taste. If an acid is added to another substance it can make it sour too. See what happens when you add lemon juice, which contains citric acid, to a glass of fresh milk, which is only very slightly acidic.

Lemon juice

Fresh milk

1 Taste the milk. Then add drops of lemon juice and stir the milk until it begins to thicken. How does it taste now?

2 Keep adding lemon juice and stirring the mixture. What happens to the milk?

What the acid does

When you add citric acid to fresh milk, it makes it strongly acidic. That is why the milk turned sour. As you add more acid, it changes the chemicals in the milk so they separate into solid curds and liquid whey.

Make your own yogurt

If you leave milk in a warm place instead of a refrigerator, minute bacteria will develop in it. These bacteria produce lactic acid which turns the milk sour. Here is a way to make yogurt by controlling this process. You will need some long-life milk,* a vacuum flask and a small amount of fresh plain yogurt, which already contains the bacteria, to get the process started.

⚠ Wash your hands thoroughly, and make sure that all your equipment is really clean before you prepare food. Take great care with hot liquids.

Long-life milk

1

Heat 250ml (8fl oz) of long-life milk in a saucepan until it starts to boil. Turn off the heat. Now pre-heat a vacuum flask by filling it with boiling water and then emptying it again.

Milk and yogurt

Warmed vacuum flask

2

Stir two teaspoons of plain yogurt into the milk, pour the mixture into the flask and screw on its lid. Leave the mixture in the flask for seven hours so the bacteria can make lactic acid.

Yogurt

Cold water

3

Pour the yogurt into a bowl. Stand the bowl in a basin of cold water and keep stirring the yogurt so that it cools quickly. This will stop the bacteria from making any more lactic acid.

Plate

4

Cover the bowl with a plate and put it in the refrigerator. Leave it to thicken for four hours. Now you can eat your yogurt on its own or mixed with fresh fruit or a spoonful of honey.

You can also use pasteurized milk, but boil it thoroughly before adding the yogurt.

Acid attack

Did you know that many buildings are attacked or corroded by acid? Fumes from factories, power stations and traffic all contain acids that are released into the atmosphere and fall as acid rain. Try this test to see how acid affects building materials.

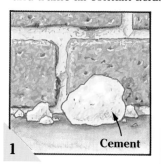

1 Look for a small lump of cement on a path or at the bottom of an old brick wall.

Cement

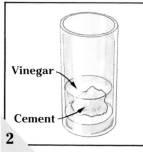

Vinegar

Cement

2 Put the cement in a glass and pour in vinegar (ethanoic acid), to cover the cement.

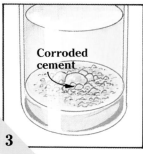

Corroded cement

3 Leave your experiment for two to three days. What happens to the cement?

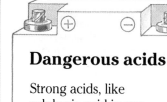

Dangerous acids

Strong acids, like sulphuric acid in car batteries, can corrode metal and eat away at human skin. Keep away from chemicals marked "acid" or "corrosive".

Make an acid indicator

You can find out if a substance contains acid by testing it with something called an indicator which changes colour when it is mixed with an acid. Follow the instructions below to make your own indicator from half a red cabbage, then use it for the experiments on the next three pages.

You will need

Half a red cabbage
Knife
Large non-enamel saucepan
Wooden spoon
Large screw-top jar
Sieve

Acid test

Once you have made your red cabbage indicator, you can use it to test for acids. Try testing aspirin, yogurt, water, orange squash, sugar, lemonade, flour or apple juice. (Only some of them contain acid.)*

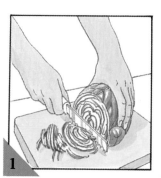

1 Carefully chop the cabbage into small pieces. Put the pieces in the saucepan with enough water to cover them.

2 Bring the water to the boil. Turn off the heat, stir the cabbage mixture and leave it to cool for 30 minutes.

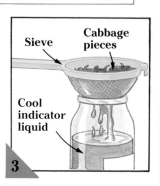

Sieve

Cabbage pieces

Cool indicator liquid

3 Pour the cabbage water through the sieve into the jar. The liquid in the jar is your indicator. Keep it in the refrigerator.

Pour some indicator into the bottom of a glass. Stir in a few drops or some crumbled bits of the substance that you want to test. If the indicator turns pink, the substance contains acid.

* *Check your results on page 60.*

COLOURFUL REACTIONS

The experiments on these two pages will help you find out more about a group of chemicals called alkalis. You can also see how alkalis react with acids.* All the experiments use red cabbage indicator, so turn back one page and make some first.

Toothpaste test

Red cabbage indicator liquid turns pink when it is mixed with acids (see the "Acid test" on page 25). The indicator also reacts with another group of chemicals called alkalis. Try the test below to see this for yourself.

1 Cover the bottom of a glass with toothpaste. Add a few drops of indicator liquid and stir the mixture thoroughly.

2 Now wait for five minutes. The indicator should slowly turn green because toothpaste is an alkali. Did your indicator go green?

Alkalis at home

Alkalis are a group of chemicals that make some things dissolve and are often used for cleaning. Toothpaste and liquid floor cleaner are alkaline. So are some indigestion remedies, and bicarbonate of soda, which is used for baking.

Strong alkalis can burn your skin. Keep all alkalis away from your eyes.

Red cabbage dye

Here is a way to use red cabbage indicator to dye a white handkerchief three different colours. You need lemon juice and bicarbonate of soda to react with the indicator and produce the colours.

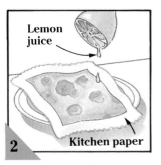

1 Soak the handkerchief in a bowl of indicator liquid for five minutes until it turns pale purple. Then dry the handkerchief between two sheets of kitchen paper.

2 Cover a plate with kitchen paper and lay the handkerchief on top. Squeeze a few drops of lemon juice onto the handkerchief. What happens?

3 Change the kitchen paper. Now mix a teaspoon of bicarbonate of soda with a little water to make a solution. Drop it onto the handkerchief. What happens now?

4 Leave the handkerchief for five minutes so the chemicals can react together. Rinse the handkerchief quickly in cold running water and hang it up to dry.

How the dye works

The acid in lemon juice turns the indicator dye pink. The alkali in bicarbonate of soda turns it green.

Now try this

Simmer a cotton T-shirt for an hour in a saucepan of water mixed with a tablespoon of alum, which is sold by chemists. Then dye it as shown above. Alum makes the dye more permanent.

See pages 24-25 for more about acids.

Red cabbage cocktails

In this surprising experiment, three glasses of clear liquid turn different colours when you add ice-cubes made from red cabbage indicator.

Prepare the ice-cubes and "drinks" in advance and then amaze your friends, but don't drink the liquids, as they will taste disgusting.

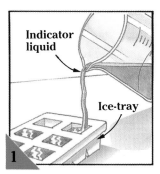

Indicator liquid

Ice-tray

1

Pour red cabbage indicator liquid into six compartments of an ice-tray. Freeze the liquid for about an hour until it forms ice-cubes.

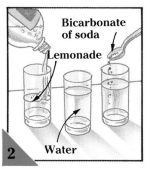

Bicarbonate of soda

Lemonade

2

Water

Fill three tall glasses, one with water, one with clear lemonade* and one with water mixed with a teaspoon of bicarbonate of soda.

Lemonade

Bicarbonate of soda and water

3

Water

Now drop two indicator ice-cubes into each glass. How do the "drinks" change? What colour are they when the ice has completely dissolved?

Why the cocktails change colour

Lemonade is acidic so the indicator turns pink.

Bicarbonate of soda is alkaline so the indicator turns blue-green. (To make it really green, add more bicarbonate.)

Water is neutral (neither acidic nor alkaline) so the indicator stays purple.

Mixing acids and alkalis

Something surprising happens when you mix acids and alkalis. Try this experiment with lemon juice, bicarbonate of soda, and red cabbage indicator to show what happens to the chemicals.

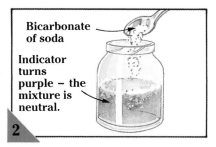

Indicator turns pink – lemon juice is acidic.

Lemon juice

1

Half fill a glass jar with red cabbage indicator liquid. Keep adding drops of lemon juice and stirring the mixture until the indicator changes colour.

Bicarbonate of soda

Indicator turns purple – the mixture is neutral.

2

Sprinkle in bicarbonate of soda. The alkali in the powder will react with the acid in the lemon juice and start fizzing.** What happens to the indicator?

How they mix

When you add an alkali to an acid, it cancels out, or neutralizes the acid. That is why the pink indicator turned purple again.

Now try this

Add more bicarbonate of soda to the neutral mixture from the last experiment. What happens? Can you turn the mixture purple again?

Curing stomach ache

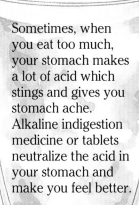

Sometimes, when you eat too much, your stomach makes a lot of acid which stings and gives you stomach ache. Alkaline indigestion medicine or tablets neutralize the acid in your stomach and make you feel better.

Instead of clear lemonade, you could use water mixed with lemon juice.
**See page 6 to find out why the mixture fizzes.*

27

CURIOUS COLOURS

Light from the sun or from a bulb looks white, but it is really made up of seven different colours: red, orange, yellow, green, blue, indigo and violet. These are the colours of a rainbow. Try the experiments here to find out more about light and colour.

Make a rainbow

When sunlight shines through raindrops it splits into its separate colours and you see a rainbow. You can make the same thing happen in a dark room, using a torch, a clear plastic box full of water, and a mirror.

1 Give your torch a narrow beam by taping on a black paper cover with a small slit in it.

2 Half fill the box with water. Stand the mirror in the water so it leans against the end of the box.

3 Point your torch so the light beam shines on the mirror under the water.

4 Hold up a white card so reflected light from the mirror shines on it. What do you see?

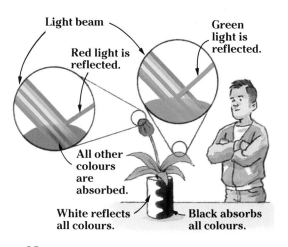

Tape
Narrow slit
Black paper
Rainbow

Why you see a rainbow

When light enters water, it slows down and bends.* All the colours that make up light travel at different speeds, so they each bend at a slightly different angle. This makes the light separate into seven colours. The mirror reflects them so you see a rainbow or spectrum.

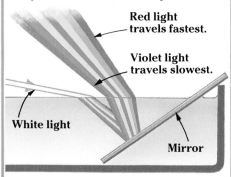

Red light travels fastest.

Violet light travels slowest.

White light

Mirror

Seeing colours

When you see colours, you are really seeing reflected light. Pure red things, for example, absorb all the colours of light except red. They reflect red light back so you see them as red. White objects look very bright because they reflect all the colours of light. Black things do not reflect any colours.

Light beam
Red light is reflected.
Green light is reflected.
All other colours are absorbed.
White reflects all colours.
Black absorbs all colours.

Seeing red

If you hold a piece of red cellophane over a picture, it acts as a filter and stops all light except red light from reaching your eyes.

Colours that do not reflect any red light, such as green and blue, look dark, but colours that reflect red look bright.

First look at the picture above to see how a red filter changes the way you see different colours. Then try to identify the object hidden in the pattern on the right. Hold a piece of red cellophane over it to see if you were right.

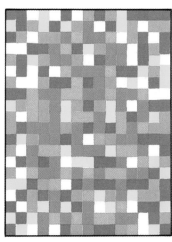

__This is refraction. See page 18 to find out more about it.__

Mixing colours

When you mix coloured paints, you get some very different results from when you mix coloured light.

Try mixing paints and then light to see what colours you make.

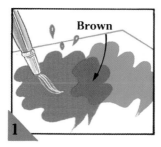

1 Use a paintbrush to mix equal amounts of red and green paint on white paper. What colour do you get?

2 Cover two torches of equal strength with pieces of red and green cellophane, fixed with elastic bands.

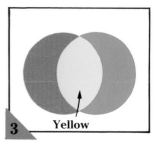

3 Shine the torches onto a white surface. What colour do you see where the red and green light overlap?

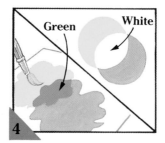

4 Now mix blue and yellow paint and then blue and yellow light. Do you get the same result with coloured paint and light?

How light mixes

White light is a mixture of all the colours of light, so when you add one coloured light to another, you get closer to white. Red, green and blue are the primary colours of light. This means you can mix them in different proportions to make light of any colour.

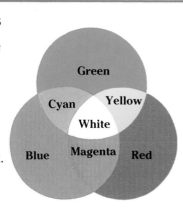

How paints mix

Coloured paints absorb all the colours of the rainbow except the ones that they reflect. So each time you add one colour paint to another, you get closer to black, which does not reflect any colours. Printers mix magenta, cyan and yellow to make all their colours.

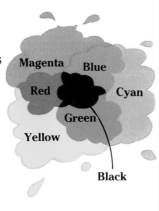

Make a rainbow spinner

Here is a way to see what happens when you mix seven colours of light together. Make this rainbow spinner, then spin it fast and watch carefully.

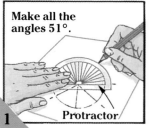

Make all the angles 51°.

1 Stand a yogurt pot upside down on a piece of cardboard and draw around it. Divide the circle into seven equal sections. Use a protractor to do this accurately.

Protractor

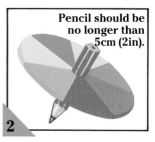

Pencil should be no longer than 5cm (2in).

2 Fill in each section with a colour of the rainbow, in the order shown here. Cut out the circle and push a short, pointed pencil through the middle of it. Now spin it fast.

What you see

When the spinner moves fast, you see light reflected from all its colours, but your brain cannot separate them. So you see a mixture of all seven colours, which is white.

Your spinner may look grey because your colours are not pure.

29

GRIPPING AND SLIDING

Whenever one surface moves across another, the force of friction works to stop it. Friction is very useful, the tyres of your bicycle couldn't grip the ground without it.

But it also creates problems, when it slows down the moving parts of machines. On these two pages you can find out more about friction and how to overcome it.

Friction's grip

Most bicycle tyres have a patterned texture or tread with many small surfaces that push against the ground to give the bike a strong grip. Try this experiment to see what happens when lots of surfaces press against each other. You need a table knife and a small plastic bottle that you have packed as tightly as you can with uncooked rice.

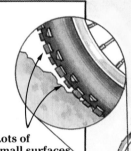

Lots of small surfaces help tyres grip.

Ball-bearings help wheels spin.

Ball-bearings help handlebars turn.

Ball-bearings help pedals work.

Ball-bearings

1 Slide the knife into the bottle full of rice until the blade and half the handle are buried in rice.

2 Jiggle the knife and squeeze the bottle, then pack in more rice until the bottle is completely full.

3 Lift the knife slowly. If the rice is packed tightly enough, friction between all the surfaces will make the rice stay in the bottle and the knife stay in the rice.

Spinning around

One way to reduce unwanted friction between moving parts is to put ball-bearings between them. Ball-bearings allow the parts to move, but stop them from rubbing against each other. To see the difference that ball-bearings make, stand a can on a smooth table-top and try to make it spin on its base. Then try this.

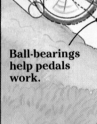

Wheel hub

Ball-bearings

You will need

Marbles (about 14)
Thin cardboard
Sticky tape
Can
Patterned paper

1 Tape a cardboard strip around the top of the can to make a collar. The collar should be deep enough to hold the marbles, with their tops just showing.

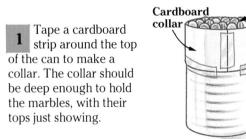

Cardboard collar

Marbles

Sticky tape

2 Tape the patterned paper around the can. Stand the can on its collar and carefully feed marbles underneath it. Now try to spin the can and watch what happens.

Patterned paper

Marbles

Adding oil

Machines run smoothly when their moving parts are covered with a thin layer of oil. The oil lubricates the parts and stops them from rubbing against each other. To see how oil works, try this test with a plastic tray, a bottle top and some cooking oil.

1 Flick the bottle top with your finger and thumb so it skims across the tray. How soon does friction make it stop?

2 Cover the tray with a thin film of oil. Then skim the bottle top across it again. How far does it travel now?

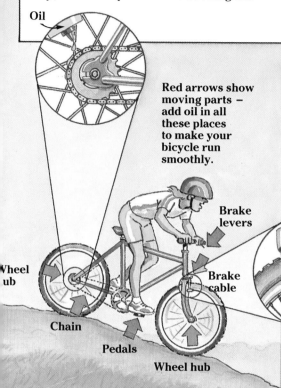

Oil

Red arrows show moving parts – add oil in all these places to make your bicycle run smoothly.

Wheel hub

Chain

Pedals

Brake levers

Brake cable

Wheel hub

Putting on the brakes

When you use your bicycle brakes, you make the brake blocks push so hard against the wheels that friction stops them from turning. When you release your brakes, there is less friction and the wheels can turn again. Here is a way to make a matchbox on a thread stop and start by "putting on the brakes" and then taking them off again.

Brake cable

Brake block pushes on wheel rim.

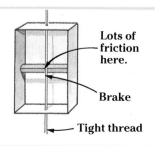

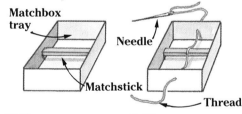

Matchbox tray

Needle

Matchstick

Thread

Picture on lid

1 Cut a matchstick to fit exactly across a matchbox tray. Wedge it in like this.

2 Use a needle to pass a thread through the tray and over the matchstick.

3 Replace the matchbox lid. Hold the thread tight, then slack. What happens?

Why the can spins

The rolling marbles underneath the can stop its base from rubbing on the table. Rolling creates much less friction than rubbing so the can spins more easily.

Friction stops can.

Can moves easily.

Why it works

When the thread is tight, it presses on the matchstick which acts as a brake. When the thread is slack, the brake is released.

Lots of friction here.

Brake

Tight thread

MAKING MICROBES WORK

Microbes are minute living things that are so small you can only see them under a microscope. Some microbes, like salmonella, cause dangerous diseases. But others, such as yeast, are very important for making food. The experiments here use dried yeast which you can buy in packets from a supermarket. 30g (1.5 oz) will be all you need.

Yeast comes to life

Dried yeast looks like lifeless granules, but it is really made up of millions of tiny microbes that stay inactive as long as they are cool and dry. Try adding water, sugar and warmth to yeast and see what happens.

You will need
Dried yeast
Sugar
Jug
Glass bottle
Balloon
Bowl

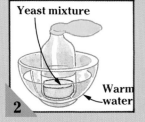

1. **Make a runny yeast mixture** in a jug by mixing two teaspoons of yeast with two tablespoons of warm water. Then stir in a teaspoon of sugar.

Sugar
Yeast mixture

2. **Pour the yeast mixture** into the bottle and stretch the balloon over its neck. Stand the bottle in a bowl of warm water for 15 minutes.

Yeast mixture
Warm water

What happens to the yeast

As the yeast feeds, it makes a gas called carbon dioxide. This fills the mixture with bubbles and blows up the balloon.

Did you know?

Wine is made by mixing yeast with sugar and fruit juice. The mixture is kept for several weeks in a special container that does not let in air. As the yeast feeds, it makes alcohol as well as carbon dioxide. The carbon dioxide gas escapes, but the alcohol turns the sugar and fruit juice into wine.

Carbon dioxide gas bubbles through here.

Make yeast work

This experiment shows what happens when you mix yeast with flour. It will take about 20 minutes to prepare, two hours for the yeast to work and 20 minutes to bake, and the result will be 12 fresh bread rolls.

Yeast mixture bubbles.

1. Pour a full mug of warm water into the jug and stir in a teaspoon of sugar. Sprinkle in two teaspoons of yeast. Wait for ten minutes. The mixture should fill with bubbles of carbon dioxide gas.

Tuck bag under bowl.

5. Put the dough back in the bowl and cover it loosely with a plastic bag. Stand the bowl by a sunny window or near a radiator. After 90 minutes, the dough should have risen to twice its original size.

Always wash your hands before you work with food.

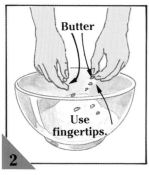

Butter

Use fingertips.

2

Pour three full mugs of flour into the mixing bowl and stir in a teaspoon of salt. Then rub in a teaspoon of butter, using your fingertips. Make a hollow in the flour and pour in the yeast mixture.

Dough

3

Use your fingers like a rake to blend the mixture into a squashy lump, called dough. Wipe the dough around the bowl to pick up all the flour. Then put it on a clean, floured surface.

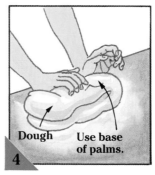

Dough **Use base of palms.**

4

Stretch, fold and punch the dough using your knuckles and palms, as shown in the picture. This is called kneading. After ten minutes, your dough should be smooth and springy.

Why you need to knead

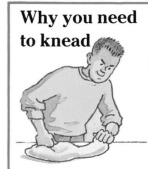

Flour contains a soft, rubbery substance which is called gluten. When you knead dough, you make the gluten into a stretchy network. This network will expand as the bread rises.

Why dough rises

When yeast feeds on sugar and flour, it makes carbon dioxide gas. This gas gets trapped in the gluten network and the dough rises.

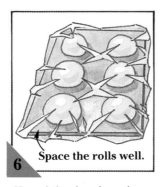

Space the rolls well.

6

Knead the dough again for three minutes, then shape it into 12 rolls. Put the rolls on baking trays that you have smeared with butter. Cover the trays with plastic bags and wait 30 minutes. The rolls should expand.

Wear oven gloves.

7

Set the oven to 230°C/450°F/gas mark 7 and wait five minutes for it to warm up. Bake the rolls for 15-20 minutes until they are crisp and brown on top, and sound hollow when tapped underneath. Cool them on a wire tray.

What happens in the oven

The heat in the oven kills the yeast and hardens the gluten network. The carbon dioxide bubbles escape, leaving the bread full of little holes.

HOW AIR PUSHES

Did you know that air presses against you all the time? On these two pages, you can see how air pushes, discover how air's pushing power, or pressure, changes when you heat it and find out what happens when you reduce the air pressure inside a container.

Paper plunge

This surprising experiment shows that the air inside a glass takes up space and pushes.

Crumple a piece of paper and push it into the bottom of a glass so it cannot fall out. Plunge the glass straight down into a bowl of water. What happens to the paper? Where is the water level in the glass?

Why the paper stays dry

Water can only get into the glass by squashing the air inside it. Air can be squashed, or compressed, a little, but then it pushes back and prevents the water from reaching the paper.

Empty the pot

For this experiment, you need a plastic pot with a tight-fitting lid, a ball-point pen and some sticky tape.

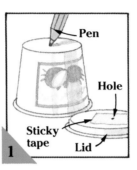

1 Make a hole in the base and lid of the pot with the ball-point pen. Cover both holes with sticky tape.

Hold pot gently.

2 Fill the pot with water and put on the lid. Gently pull the tape off the base. Does any water come out?

Tape
Hole

3 Now pull the tape off the lid. What happens? Try covering and uncovering the hole with your finger.

How the pot empties

When the hole in the lid is covered, the air below the pot pushes up harder than the water in the pot pushes down. So the water does not pour out.

Water pushes down.

Air pushes down.

Hole

Air pushes up.

When you uncover the hole in the lid, the air above it pushes down on the water in the pot. This helps it push hard enough to pour out.

Lift a friend

This scientific stunt shows the pushing power of air. It works because air from your lungs is spread over a wide area, so it can support a lot of weight.

Lay a strong plastic bag on a table so its top third hangs over the edge. Put a large book on the bag and ask a friend to sit on it. Make one end of the bag into a mouthpiece and blow into it hard. Your friend should be lifted off the table.

Jumping coin

What happens to air's push when you heat it up? Try this simple test with a glass bottle, a coin and some cold water.

1 First smear some cold water over the coin and the top of the bottle. This will make an airtight seal when you rest the coin on the bottle.

2 Rest the coin on top of the bottle. Now hold your hands around the bottle and wait for about 30 seconds. What happens to the coin?

Cold water

Coin

3 Take your hands off the bottle and wait again. What happens to the coin now?

Why the coin jumps

When you hold the bottle, the air inside it heats up. Warm air pushes harder than the cool air outside the bottle so it forces up the coin. The coin stops jumping when the air in the bottle cools down.

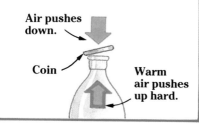

Air pushes down.

Coin

Warm air pushes up hard.

Sticking together

Here is a way to see what happens when the air inside a container pushes outwards less strongly than the air outside it pushes inwards. You will need two identical yogurt pots with flat rims, a night-light candle, matches, scissors and a 10cm (4in) square of blotting paper.

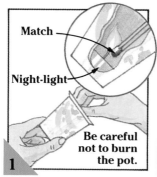

Match

Night-light

Be careful not to burn the pot.

1

Match rims exactly.

Wet blotting paper

2

3

Cut a 1.5cm (0.5in) hole in the middle of the blotting paper, then wet it thoroughly. Stand the night-light in one of the pots, tip the pot and light the night-light.

Quickly cover the pot with the wet blotting paper. Then stand the second pot upside-down on top of it, making sure that it fits exactly over the first pot.

Wait until the flame goes out (about 20 seconds). Then lift the top pot gently. If you have matched their rims exactly, the pots should stick together.

Why the pots stick together

As the night-light burns, it uses up the oxygen inside the pots.* This means that there is less air in the pots pushing out. The air outside the pots pushes inwards and holds them together.

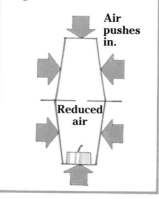

Air pushes in.

Reduced air

Did you know?

You cannot feel air pushing in on you because your body pushes outwards with the same force as the air. In outer space, where there is no air, astronauts have to wear pressurized space suits that push against their bodies with the same force as the air on earth.

See "Using oxygen" on page 7.

MOVING AIR

The experiments on the last two pages showed that air has push or pressure, but what happens to that pressure when air moves over, under or around things? Try these experiments with moving air and find out how it helps planes to fly.

Blow the apples

In 1738, a scientist called Bernoulli found that liquids and gases have less pressure when they are moving than when they are still. This is called the Bernoulli principle. You can test this principle by doing a simple experiment with moving air.

Tape two apples on strings from a door-frame so they hang about 3cm (1in) apart, and level with your mouth. Wait until the apples are steady, then blow hard between them. Do the apples move apart or together?

Why the apples move together

When you blow, you make the air between the apples move. This moving air has less pressure than the still air on either side of them. So the still air pushes the apples together.

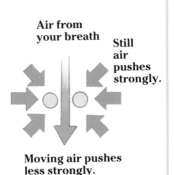

Air from your breath

Still air pushes strongly.

Moving air pushes less strongly.

Lift the card

In this surprising experiment, you make a cardboard square rise and hover in the air, just by blowing on it.

You will need

Bendy drinking straw
Plastic cotton reel *
Sticky tape
Scissors
5cm (2in) cardboard square
Drawing-pin

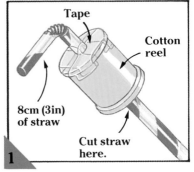

Tape

Cotton reel

8cm (3in) of straw

Cut straw here.

1

Push the straw through the cotton reel so about 8cm (3in) of straw sticks out the bottom. Tape it in place, then cut off the rest of the straw.

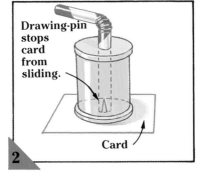

Drawing-pin stops card from sliding.

Card

2

Stick the drawing-pin through the middle of the card and stand the cotton reel over it. Blow down the straw, lift the cotton reel and watch the card.

Why the card lifts

Moving air from your breath spreads over the top of the card. The still air below the card pushes up more strongly than the moving air pushes down. So the card is pushed up against the cotton reel.

Air from your breath

Cotton reel

Moving air

Moving air

Card   Still air

Now try this

You can use the apparatus that you made in the last experiment to keep a ping-pong ball in the air. Moving air from your breath holds the ball up, while still air pushes hard around it and stops the ball from falling.

Blow here.

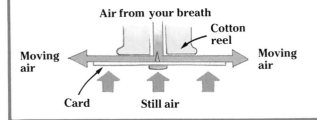

* Empty spool of thread (US).

Whistling water spray

This drinking straw spray uses the difference in pressure between moving air and still air to lift water from a saucer. As you blow into it, air and water vibrate inside the straw and make a whistling sound.*

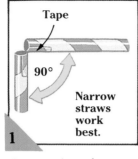

Tape

90°

Narrow straws work best.

1

Cut two pieces from a plastic drinking straw, about 3cm (1in) and 5cm (2in) long. Join the straws with sticky tape along one side so they form a 90° angle, as shown in the picture.

Spray

2

Stand the short straw upright in a saucer of water. Now blow hard and steadily through the long straw. Put your hand in front of the long straw. What do you feel?

Why it works

The moving air at the top of the upright straw pushes down less strongly than the still air above the water in the saucer. So the water is pushed up the straw and blown out as spray.

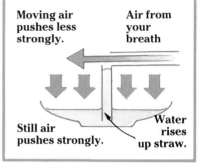

Moving air pushes less strongly.

Air from your breath

Still air pushes strongly.

Water rises up straw.

Raise the wing

Planes stay in the air because their wings have a special curved shape called an aerofoil. To see how planes' wings help them to fly, make a wing from a strip of paper and watch what happens when air travels over and under the wing.

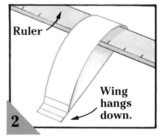

This shape is called an aerofoil.

Tape

Top

Bottom

Fold

1

Cut a paper strip about 25cm x 5cm (10in × 2in). Fold it in half, then tape the top of the wing to the bottom, about 1.5cm (0.5in) from the end.

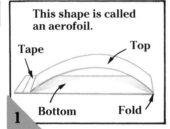

Ruler

Wing hangs down.

2

Slide your wing onto a ruler as shown in the picture. Now hold the ruler so your mouth is opposite the folded edge of the wing.

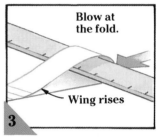

Blow at the fold.

Wing rises

3

Blow hard and steadily at the fold. The bottom of the wing should rise and the wing should keep hovering until you stop blowing on it.

How wings work

When a plane travels through the air, air moves over and under its wings, just like your breath moved over and under the paper wing.

The air that is forced over the curved tops of the wings has to travel further and faster than the air underneath them. So the slower-moving air below the wings pushes up harder than the fast-moving air above them and lifts the plane.

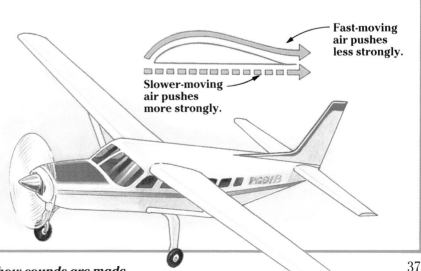

Fast-moving air pushes less strongly.

Slower-moving air pushes more strongly.

* See pages 10-11 for more about how sounds are made.

CRACK THE CRIME WITH CHEMISTRY

Detectives all over the world use chemistry to help them solve crimes. Try the experiments on these two pages and help detectives Ivor Clue and Laura Biding solve the mystery of the altered report.

IVOR SUSPECTS THAT SOMEONE HAS WRITTEN ON HIS SCHOOL REPORT.

CHEMISTRY Outstandinglybad PHYSICS Incompetent

BUT HOW CAN I PROVE IT?

NOW IVOR KNOWS HIS SCHOOL REPORT HAS BEEN ALTERED. BUT WHO DID IT?

I SUSPECT MY OLD ENEMY BETTY BADFINGER, BUT I NEED MORE EVIDENCE..

PERHAPS THESE INKY FINGERPRINTS ON THE EDGE OF MY REPORT COULD HELP?

IVOR USES INVISIBLE INK TO WRITE A SECRET MESSAGE TO LAURA, ASKING HER TO GET A SET OF BETTY'S FINGERPRINTS.

Ink test

Here is a way to tell two inks apart. Cut a 6cm (2.5in) square from coffee filter paper or blotting paper. Write a word near the bottom of the square, half with one blue felt-tip pen and half with a different one. Then try the test below.

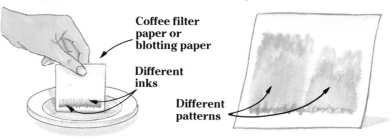

Coffee filter paper or blotting paper

Different inks

Different patterns

1 Dip the bottom of the paper square into a saucer of water, keeping the writing above the water level. Wait for the water to rise to the top of the paper. Then let the square dry.

2 The chemicals in the two inks will be carried up the paper by the rising water, leaving two different patterns. This method of separating coloured chemicals is called chromatography.

Invisible ink

For this "ink", you need six laxative pills containing the chemical phenolphthalein. This chemical is an indicator which turns pink when it is mixed with an alkali*, like washing soda.

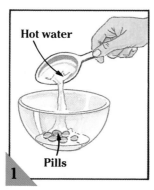

Hot water

Pills

1

False message on top

Secret message underneath

2

Washing soda solution

Secret message turns pink.

3

First soak any coloured coating off the pills. Then put the pills in a bowl, add five tablespoons of hot water, and stir until the pills dissolve. The solution you have made is your invisible ink.

Dip a blunt pencil in the ink and write your secret message on a brown envelope. Keep dipping the pencil in the ink after every letter. When the ink is dry, add a false message with a pen.

To read the message, mix four teaspoons of washing soda with four tablespoons of hot water to make a solution. Then dip a tissue in the solution and dab it over the envelope.

Be very careful with washing soda. Keep it away from your eyes, wash your hands when you have finished experimenting and keep the pills and the soda out of reach of small children.

See pages 25-27 for more about indicators and alkalis.

IVOR DELIVERS HIS SECRET MESSAGE.

I NEED SOMETHING WITH BETTY'S FINGERPINTS ON IT.

LATER AT LAURA'S HOUSE..

WHILE BETTY IS LOOKING THE OTHER WAY, LAURA GRABS HER EMPTY CARRIER BAG.

WHAT DOES LAURA DO NOW?

Taking fingerprints

Whenever you touch something, you leave slightly oily fingerprints behind. If these prints are on a shiny surface, like a plastic bag, they will show up when you cover them with fine powder. In this experiment, you make carbon powder and then use it to take a friend's fingerprints.

Don't let the toast catch fire.

Carbon

1

Toast a piece of bread until it turns black around the edges. The heat in the toaster will make the bread change into carbon.

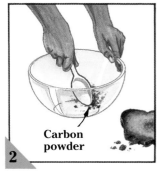

Carbon powder

2

Scrape the carbon off the toast into a bowl. Then crush it with the back of a spoon to make a very fine powder.

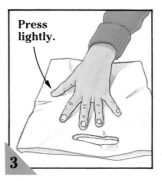

Press lightly.

3

Ask a friend to run her fingers through her hair. Then ask her to press her fingertips on a white plastic bag.

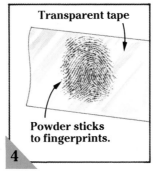

Transparent tape

Powder sticks to fingerprints.

4

Sprinkle carbon powder onto the fingerprints. Shake the excess powder off the bag and cover the prints with sticky tape.

Did you know?

Scientists help detectives to crack crimes. They use powerful microscopes to examine hairs, carpet fibres, dirt from shoes, spots of blood and even scraps of clothing left at the scene of the crime.

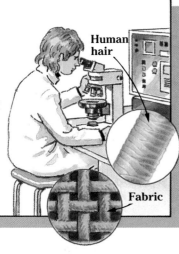

Human hair

Fabric

BETTY'S FINGERPRINTS ON THE BAG MATCH THE PRINTS ON YOUR REPORT EXACTLY!

WATCH OUT BETTY BADFINGER – WE'VE CRACKED THE CRIME AND WE'RE AFTER YOU!

HOW MOLECULES PULL

Scientists think that things are made up of tiny particles, called molecules, which pull towards each other. You cannot see these molecules, even under a microscope, but you çan see the effect of their pull on each other. Try these experiments to see how oddly water can behave, because of the way its molecules pull together.

Bulging water

Fill a glass to the brim with water. Then gently slide a coin into the glass. Look very carefully at the surface of the water. What happens to it?

How many coins can you slide in before the water overflows?

Why the water bulges

Molecules in water pull towards each other in all directions. This creates a force at the surface of the water that is strong enough to hold some water above the level of the glass. This pulling force at the surface of water is called surface tension.

Non-spilling water

For this experiment you need a coin and two equal-sized glasses or yogurt pots. Be very careful with the glasses.

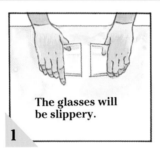

The glasses will be slippery.

1

Fill the two glasses underwater. Then take them out of the water, holding them rim-to-rim so no water escapes.

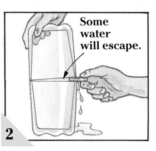

Some water will escape.

2

Stand the glasses on a flat surface so that one rests upside-down on top of the other. Slide the coin between the two rims.

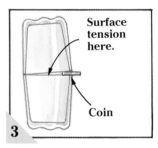

Surface tension here.

Coin

3

When the coin is in place, water molecules will pull together between the rims and stop the water overflowing.

Tie a knot in water

Here is another way to watch how water molecules pull towards each other. To try it, you need a plastic bottle with three holes pierced near the base, about 5mm (0.25in) apart. Make the holes with a drawing-pin and then a ball-point pen.

1 Fill the bottle with water and hold it over a sink.

Water spurts out of the bottle in three separate streams.

2 Pinch the streams of water together, then take your hand away.

The three streams pull together to make a single stream.

3 Now run your finger across the three holes in the bottle.

The surface tension of the single stream is broken. Three streams form again.

Did you know?

Water forms drops because its molecules pull together.

Upside-down jar

This surprising experiment shows how water molecules pull across the tiny holes in the fabric of a handkerchief. You can try the experiment on your own or do it as a trick on a friend.

1 Half fill a glass with water. Stretch a handkerchief over the top of it and fix it with an elastic band.

2 Now turn the glass upside-down. The water molecules should pull together and stop any water from falling through the holes.

3 To weaken the molecules' pull, touch the handkerchief with your finger. What happens to the water now?

Did you know?

Tents keep rain out just like the handkerchief kept the water in the glass. If you touch the inside of a tent when it is raining, you will weaken the surface tension of the water resting on it and let in the rain.

Disturbing the surface

In the last experiment, you weakened the pull of the molecules by touching the surface of water with your finger. To see exactly what happens when you disturb water's surface, try these tests with a bowl of water lightly sprinkled with talcum powder.

1 Touch the surface lightly with your finger and hold it there. What happens to the talcum powder?

2 Refill the bowl, sprinkle on powder and touch the surface with a bar of soap. What does the powder do now?

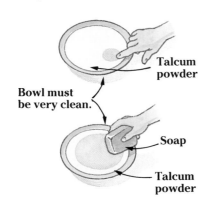

Talcum powder

Bowl must be very clean.

Soap

Talcum powder

What happens at the surface

There is oil in your skin and in soap. When oil is mixed with water, it stops the water molecules from pulling together so strongly. This is what happens when you put your finger and the soap in the bowl. Because the molecules at the edge of the bowl are still pulling strongly, the talcum powder is dragged to the edge of the bowl.

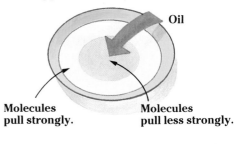

Oil

Molecules pull strongly.

Molecules pull less strongly.

Soap-propelled boat

Here is a way to make a matchstick boat travel across a bath, like the talcum powder moved across the bowl in the tests above.

Soap

Split matchstick

1 Make a small cut in the end of a matchstick with a knife. Do this very carefully.

The boat will keep moving until all the water is soapy.

2 Wedge a tiny piece of soap in the back of the matchstick boat.

3 Put the boat in the water. The soap will make the water molecules behind it pull less hard than the molecules in front of it.

FROZEN SOLID

When water is cooled to a temperature of 0°C (32°F), it freezes solid and changes into ice. Ice is a strange solid which behaves in some very surprising ways. Try the experiments on this page to find out more about it.

Water level challenge

Float an ice-cube in a glass of water mixed with food colouring. Mark the water level with a strip of sticky tape. Can you predict where the water level will be when the ice-cube has melted?

Tape shows water level.

What happens to the water level

Even though part of the ice-cube floats above the surface, the water level in the glass is the same before and after the ice has melted. This shows that when ice melts, the water formed takes up less space than the ice.

Make a hole in ice

Put a pinch of salt on the middle of an ice-cube. Leave it in a cool place for ten minutes. What happens to the cube?

Salt

How you make the hole

Ice does not melt until it reaches 0°C (32°F), which is its melting point. When you add salt to ice, the salt lowers the melting point of the ice, so that it does not have to reach 0°C (32°F) to melt. That is why the salty middle of the ice-cube changes into water, while the outside of the cube stays frozen.

Salty ice melts first.

Pure ice stays frozen longer.

Sinking through ice

Here is another way to melt ice without heating it. You will need a piece of thin wire about 20cm (8in) long, some sticky tape, a bottle, and some weights, such as spoons.

Wind the ends of the wire around the handles of two heavy spoons and fix them with tape. Balance the ice-cube on the top of the bottle. Rest the wire across the cube so the spoons hang down equally on either side. Now watch what happens.

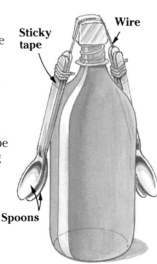

Sticky tape

Wire

Spoons

How it works

Pressure lowers the melting point of ice, so it changes into water where the wire presses on it. As the wire sinks through the ice, the water above it freezes again.

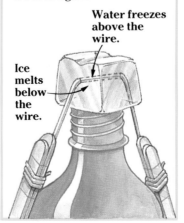

Water freezes above the wire.

Ice melts below the wire.

Did you know?

Ice-skaters really skate on water, not ice. Their weight presses on the ice, making it change into water under their skates as they glide along.

CRYSTAL GAZING

If you look at some salt grains through a magnifying glass, you will see that they all have the same shape, with straight edges and flat surfaces. This regular shape is called a crystal. Lots of substances, including sugar and diamonds, form crystals. On this page, you can learn how to grow your own crystal and find out more about how crystals are made.

 Always treat chemicals with care. Wash your hands after you have handled them and keep them away from young children.

Grow a crystal in a jar

Here is a way to grow a crystal from alum, which you can buy from a chemist's shop. The experiment uses about 200g (7oz) of alum powder and takes about three weeks. In the first week, you make a tiny crystal to use as a seed. In the next two weeks, you grow a much larger crystal around your seed.

Making the seed

1 Pour 600ml (1pt) of water into a saucepan. Measure 100g (4oz) of alum into a jug and pour it into the saucepan. Heat the mixture gently, and stir it. Then add extra alum until no more will dissolve.

2 Let the alum solution cool, then pour some into a saucer and the rest into a glass jar. Stir a tablespoon of alum into the jar, making a saturated solution. Cover the jar with a cloth.

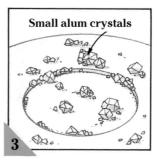

3 Meanwhile, stand the saucer in a cool, dry place. After a few days, small crystals will form. Leave them until all the solution has evaporated, then choose the biggest as your seed.

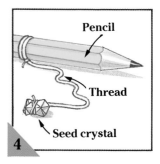

4 Carefully tie a long thread around your seed crystal. Then wind the other end of the thread around a pencil. Remove the cover from the jar of saturated solution. You are ready to grow your crystal.

Growing the crystal

Balance the pencil over the jar so the seed crystal hangs in the saturated solution. The crystal should grow for about two weeks. When it stops, take it out of the jar and keep it in a small matchbox, wrapped in a paper tissue.

Check your crystal every day. If it starts to shrink, the solution in the jar is too weak. Reheat it and add more alum to make it stronger.

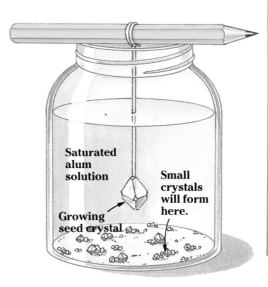

Saturated alum solution

Small crystals will form here.

Growing seed crystal

How the crystal grows

The seed crystals are formed as the water in the saucer evaporates and tiny particles of alum join together.

The crystal in the jar keeps growing as the water evaporates. The solution gets stronger and alum particles crystallize around the seed crystal.

EARTH, SUN AND MOON

Why do shadows move during the day? Why does the Sun look red at sunrise and sunset? What happens at an eclipse of the Sun? The experiments on these two pages will help you answer these questions and discover more about the Earth in space.

Make a shadow clock

Shadows on the Earth keep moving because the Earth is always spinning. This shadow clock will help you find out about the way the Earth spins. You can also use it to tell the time, but each day it will be slightly less accurate as the Sun rises at a different time.

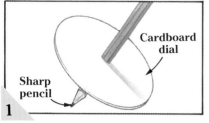

1 Cut a circle from stiff cardboard to make a dial. Push a sharp pencil through the middle of it.

Cardboard dial

Sharp pencil

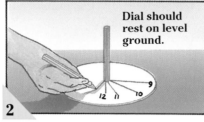

2 Push the pencil into the ground. Mark on the dial where the pencil's shadow falls each hour.

Dial should rest on level ground.

Why shadows move

The pencil's shadow moves steadily across the dial, showing that the earth spins at a steady speed. Shadows are long in the early morning and late afternoon because the Sun is low in the sky. At midday, when the Sun is overhead, they are very short.

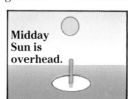

Morning Sun is low in the sky.

Midday Sun is overhead.

Evening Sun is low in the sky.

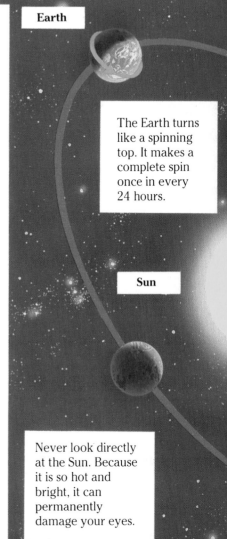

Earth

The Earth turns like a spinning top. It makes a complete spin once in every 24 hours.

Sun

Never look directly at the Sun. Because it is so hot and bright, it can permanently damage your eyes.

Sunset in a box

Here is a way to see why the Sun looks red at sunrise and sunset, but yellowy-white all the rest of the day. Fill a see-through plastic box with water and add a teaspoon of milk. Then try this experiment.

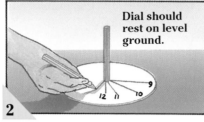

Torch

Light looks yellowy-white.

Plastic box

Milky water

1 Shine a torch straight downwards. This is like the Sun at midday.

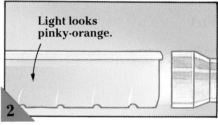

Light looks pinky-orange.

2 Shine the torch sideways through the box. This is like the setting Sun.

This simplified diagram of the Sun, Earth and Moon should help you understand the experiments here. You can see the Earth in four different positions on its yearly journey around the Sun.

Moon

The Moon travels around the Earth about once every month.

Make an eclipse of the Sun

Because the Earth moves around the Sun and the Moon moves around the Earth, the Moon sometimes passes between the Sun and the Earth. This is called an eclipse. You can make a model eclipse, using a torch for the Sun, an orange for the Earth, and a ball of plasticine, about a quarter of the size of the "Earth", for the Moon.

1 Stand the "Earth" and the "Moon" on a table with the Moon about 20cm (8in) in front of the Earth.

2 Shine your "Sun" torch directly at the Moon and Earth from about 60cm (2ft) away.

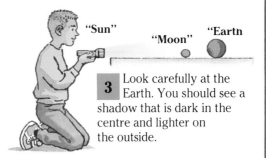

"Sun"   "Moon"   "Earth"

3 Look carefully at the Earth. You should see a shadow that is dark in the centre and lighter on the outside.

What happens in an eclipse

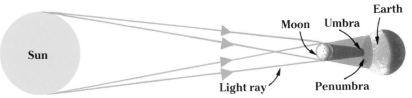

Sun   Moon   Umbra   Earth

Light ray   Penumbra

The Moon blocks out the Sun's rays and casts a double shadow on the surface of the Earth. The dark centre is called the umbra. The lighter outer shadow is called the penumbra.

What you see at an eclipse

From the umbra you see a total eclipse. Only the Sun's outer atmosphere is visible.

From the penumbra you see a partial eclipse. The Sun is partly covered by the Moon.

Why the Sun looks red

The Earth is surrounded by a blanket of air, called the atmosphere, which is filled with dust particles. These particles behave like the milk in the water and scatter light.

Sun's rays at midday

Sun's rays at sunrise   Sun's rays at sunset

Earth's atmosphere

Earth

At sunrise and sunset, sunlight travels further through the atmosphere so more of it is scattered. The red and orange parts of sunlight are hardest to scatter so more of them reach the earth.

THIRSTY PLANTS

The experiments here explore what happens when you give plants water. Some of them take less than an hour, but others take a few days.

Watching the water

This two part experiment shows what happens when you water a wilting plant. You will see your first result in 30 minutes and your second after 24 hours.

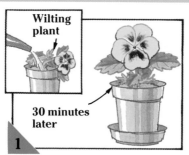

1 Water the soil around the plant. Then wait 30 minutes.

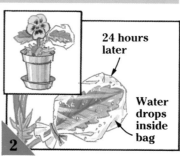

2 Tie a plastic bag over a leaf. Look at it after 24 hours.

Where the water goes

Plants absorb water through their roots and suck it up into their leaves, which transpire, sending out water droplets.

Self-watering garden

Look in your garden or street for small, damp-loving plants to fill this garden in a jar. You should find several sorts of moss and ferns growing in damp corners and walls.

You will need

Large jar with airtight lid
Gravel
Crumbly soil
Ruler
Small plants and moss
2 long sticks – for planting

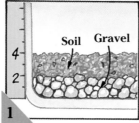

1 Pour 2cm (0.75in) of gravel into the jar, then add an equal layer of soil. Use a stick to make holes for the plants, leaving some space between them.

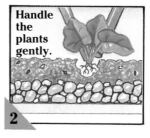

2 Lower in the plants, using the two sticks. Push down the soil around them and add the moss. Now pour in water until the soil is soaked.

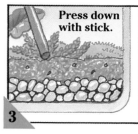

3 Press down on the soil again and leave the jar open for three days, so some water evaporates. Replace the lid and watch your plants grow.*

How it grows

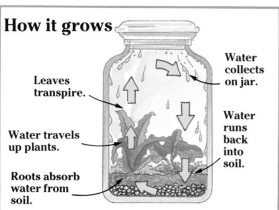

Water collects on jar.

Leaves transpire.

Water travels up plants.

Water runs back into soil.

Roots absorb water from soil.

Did you know?

Trees and plants in rain forests help to make rain in the same way as your garden in a jar waters itself. If a forest is cut down, the area around it may suffer from drought.

Leaves transpire. Rainclouds form. Rain falls.

Trees and plants absorb water.

Remove the lid for one hour, once a week.

Two colour celery

In this experiment, you can see how water travels through the stalk of a plant and into its leaves. To try it, you will need a leafy celery stalk, some red and blue food colouring, scissors and two yogurt pots with their tops cut off.

1 Use the scissors to cut up the middle of the celery stalk. Stand the split stalk in the yogurt pots in a warm, light place.

2 Half fill the pots with water and add a few drops of food colouring: red in one pot and blue in the other.

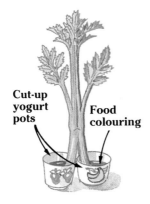

Cut-up yogurt pots

Food colouring

3 Look at the celery after an hour. What has happened to the stalk? Leave your experiment for 12 hours and then look at it again. What do the leaves look like now?

Why the celery changes colour

As the celery leaves transpire, water is pulled up the stalk and into the leaves, through narrow canals called xylem vessels. Because each vessel leads to a different part of the plant, half the leaves turn red and the other half turn blue.

Xylem vessels carry water.

Sprouting seeds

It takes less than a week to grow sprouts from lentils and all you need to give them is water. They taste good in salads and sandwiches and are full of vitamin C. You can buy lentils at a health food shop, or you might find some in your kitchen cupboard at home.

You will need
Green or brown lentils
Tall glass jar
Pop sock or cut-up tights *
Elastic band

Lentils

1 **Water**

Half fill the jar with water and add two teaspoons of lentils. Leave the jar in a warm place overnight, so the lentils can absorb the water.

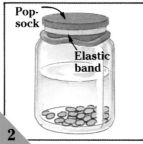

Pop-sock

Elastic band

2

In the morning, stretch the pop-sock over the jar and fix it with an elastic band. Turn the jar upside-down to strain out the water.

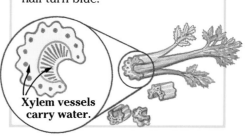

Cold water

3

Keep the jar with the damp lentils in a warm, dark place. Rinse the lentils three times a day by pouring water into the jar and straining it.

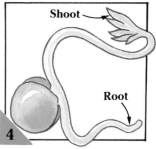

Shoot

Root

4

In three to six days, the lentil sprouts should have shoots and roots. When the sprouts measure 5cm (2in), they are ready to wash and eat.

Why seeds sprout

All seeds contain two important parts: a food store and an embryo. You can see these parts in the picture on the right. When you soak sprouting seeds in water and leave them in the dark, they start to grow, or germinate. The embryo uses the food store for energy and pushes out a shoot and a root.

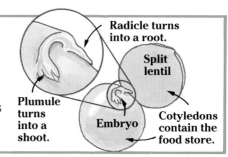

Radicle turns into a root.

Split lentil

Plumule turns into a shoot.

Embryo

Cotyledons contain the food store.

WARMING UP

The investigations on this page and on the page opposite explore the effects of heat and cold on water and air. These experiments will help you understand more about wind and rain before you make the weather station shown on pages 50-51.

Warm water fountain

You can do this experiment with a large bowl or in a sink full of cold water.

You will need

Plastic pot with lid
Ball-point pen
Small stones
Large bowl
Food colouring

1

2

3

Make two holes in the plastic pot with your ball-point pen: one in the lid of the pot and one in the side near the base of the pot. Fill the bowl or the sink with cold water.

Cover the hole in the pot with your thumb and fill it to the brim with warm water. Add a few drops of food colouring to the water. Then put the lid on the pot.

Stand the pot in the bowl of water and put stones on its lid to hold it down. Make sure that the hole in the lid is uncovered. What happens to the coloured water?

How the fountain works

When liquids are heated, they expand and become less dense. This makes them rise above cooler liquids. As they cool, they become more dense and sink down again. That is why the warm water rose out of the top of the pot into the cold water, and then slowly sank towards the bottom of the bowl.

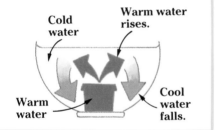

Warm air propeller

This simple paper propeller is driven by the warmth from your hand. This warmth heats the air around your hand. The air rises as it becomes warm, and then falls as it cools, just like the water in the experiment above.

Trace the propeller shape on page 61 onto a piece of thin writing paper. Cut out your propeller and make a crease along the dotted line. Unfold it and balance it on a pencil point in the middle of the crease line. Now watch it spin.

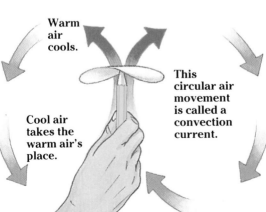

Did you know?

Huge convection currents in the Earth's atmosphere help to make our winds. This simplified diagram shows how air warms and rises, and then cools and falls, creating currents of air.

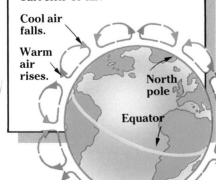

WATER IN THE AIR

The air is full of invisible water vapour. When this vapour meets something very cold, it changes into water. This is called condensation. When water heats up, the opposite happens and it changes into vapour. This is evaporation. The experiment below uses evaporation and condensation and will help you understand the way that rain is made.

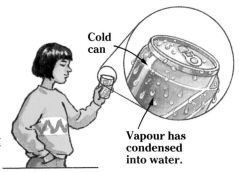

Cold can

Vapour has condensed into water.

Make pure water

When you boil water, you make it evaporate very fast. This experiment shows you how to change boiling salty water into pure water, using evaporation and condensation.

1 Carefully pour about 2cm (0.75in) of boiling water into the large bowl. Stir in three tablespoons of salt and some food colouring.

2 Stand the small bowl in the middle of the coloured water. If it floats, tip some water out of the large bowl.

3 Cover the large bowl with the plastic wrap. Put the coin in the middle of the plastic wrap, over the small bowl.

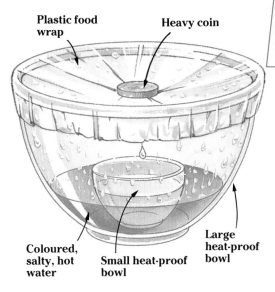

Plastic food wrap

Heavy coin

Coloured, salty, hot water

Small heat-proof bowl

Large heat-proof bowl

You will need

Large heat-proof bowl
Salt
Food colouring
Plastic food wrap
Small heat-proof bowl
Heavy coin

4 After two hours, some water will have collected inside the small bowl. What colour is it? Does it taste salty?

⚠️ The water collected in this experiment is safe to taste, because it is made from boiled drinking water. Never taste water that might be impure.

How you make pure water

Water vapour from the boiling salty water rises until it meets the plastic wrap where it cools and condenses into pure water. The pure water runs down the plastic wrap and drips into the small bowl. This process is called distillation.

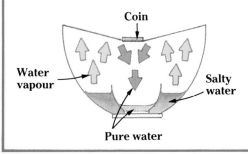

Coin

Water vapour

Salty water

Pure water

Did you know?

Rain is made by distillation. Heat from the sun makes water evaporate from oceans, rivers and lakes. The warm water vapour rises until it meets colder air where it condenses into water droplets and forms clouds. When the droplets get too heavy to stay in the air, they fall as rain.

Water vapour

Rain

WEATHER WATCHING

Here is a weather station to set up outside. You can use the instruments shown below to compare wind speeds, measure daily rainfall and see how the temperature changes during the day. To find out more about wind and rain, turn back to pages 48-49.

Watch the wind

When the wind blows on the plastic sails of this simple instrument, it makes them spin around. By counting the number of spins in a fixed time, you can record the wind's speed. Then you can see how it changes from day to day.

You will need

Large plastic bottle
Scissors
Sticky tape
Empty pen case
Brightly coloured
sticky tape
Thin knitting needle

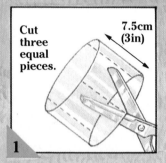

Cut three equal pieces.

7.5cm (3in)

1

Cut a 7.5cm (3in) section from the middle of the plastic bottle. Cut it into three parts and trim them to the same size. These are the sails.

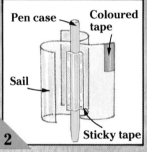

Pen case

Coloured tape

Sail

Sticky tape

2

Tape the sails to the empty pen case. Stick a piece of coloured tape to the top corner of one sail, so you can watch it as the sails spin.

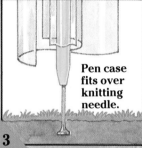

Pen case fits over knitting needle.

3

Push the blunt end of the knitting needle into the ground. Slip the pen case over the needle, so that its top rests on the needle's point.

DAYS	SPINS
MON	20
TUE	9
WED	4
THU	7
FRI	32
SAT	12
SUN	8

4

Each day, count the number of times that the wind makes the sails spin in a fixed time, such as 30 seconds. Record your results in a notebook.

Measure rainfall

All you need to measure daily rainfall is a round glass jar, with a paper scale taped to its side, and a funnel made from the top of a plastic bottle.

The scale measures the amount of rain that falls on the area covered by the bottom of the jar. Make sure the top of your funnel is the same size as the bottom of the jar, so you get an accurate measurement. Empty the jar after recording the rainfall each day.

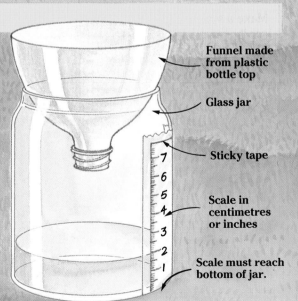

Funnel made from plastic bottle top

Glass jar

Sticky tape

Scale in centimetres or inches

Scale must reach bottom of jar.

Make a bottle thermometer

This thermometer works because water expands as it heats up and contracts as it cools down. First make and test your thermometer, then make your own scale for it. Your scale will not measure temperature in centigrade or fahrenheit, but it will show you how the temperature rises and falls at different times of day.

You will need

Glass bottle
Food colouring
Narrow drinking
    straw
Plasticine
Bowl
Cardboard
Ball-point pen
Sticky tape

Food colouring

Glass bottle

Cold water

1

Fill a glass bottle with cold water. Add some drops of food colouring to the water, then top up the bottle with water until it overflows.

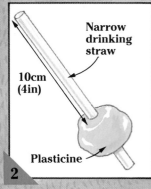

Narrow drinking straw

10cm (4in)

Plasticine

2

Roll a strip of plasticine around the straw so that 10cm (4in) of straw sticks over the top. Be careful not to crush the straw when you do this.

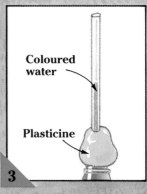

Coloured water

Plasticine

3

Push the plasticine around the top of the bottle, making sure no air can escape from the sides. Some water will rise up the straw.

Water in straw expands.

Water may overflow.

Warm water

4

Stand the bottle in a bowl of warm water for five minutes. Then take it out again. The water in the straw should rise and then fall.

Using the thermometer

Make a scale from a cardboard strip 12cm x 5cm or 4.75in x 2in. Mark the strip at 1cm or 0.5in intervals and number the markings 1-10. Tape the scale to the drinking straw. Stand the bottle thermometer in the shade outside and record the water level in the straw at different times of the day.

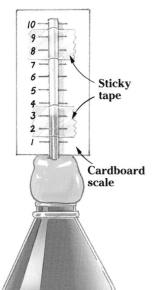

Sticky tape

Cardboard scale

You can show changes in temperature on a chart like the one below.

Scale on your bottle thermometer

Times of the day

8 AM 10 AM 12 AM 3 PM 6 PM

MAGNETIC ATTRACTIONS

If you hold a steel paper-clip close to a magnet, you can feel the magnet pulling on the paper-clip with an invisible force called magnetism. The experiments with magnets on these two pages will help you to find out more about the way magnetism works and how it can be passed on to some other objects. Look for magnets in old toys or on fridge stickers, or buy a bar or horseshoe magnet from a toy shop.

Testing the pull

Is the force of magnetism strong enough to travel through things? Try these tests with a magnet and a paper-clip.

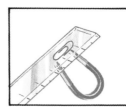

Draw a maze on a piece of cardboard. Can you guide a paper-clip through the maze?

Can you rescue a paper-clip from a glass of water without getting wet?

Will the paper-clip climb the ruler? (You can use a plastic or a wooden ruler.)

How magnets pull

Magnets pull on magnetic materials, such as iron and steel, but pull through non-magnetic things, like cardboard, glass, plastic and wood. Magnetism even travels through water.

Make needle-magnets

Magnetism can be passed from magnets to other magnetic materials so they become magnets too. Here is a way to magnetize two needles. You will need the needle-magnets for other experiments here.

1 Hold a needle by the eye and stroke it gently 30 times with your magnet, in the same direction. Now do the same with the second needle, making sure that you use the same end of the magnet.

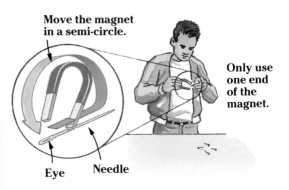

Move the magnet in a semi-circle.

Only use one end of the magnet.

Eye   **Needle**

2 Test your needle-magnets on some pins, before you use them for other experiments.

Pulling and pushing

When you put two magnets together, they behave in surprising ways. To see how magnets react together, rest your two needle-magnets on small pieces of paper in a bowl of water. Then watch them pull and push.

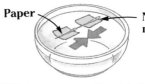

Paper   **Needle-magnet**

1 Float the needles side by side with one point beside the other eye. What happens?

2 Put the needles eye to eye. What happens to them now?

Why magnets pull and push

All magnets have two ends, or poles. If you put the poles of two magnets together, they will either pull together or push apart. They will pull, or attract each other, if the poles are different. They will push, or repel each other, if the poles are the same.

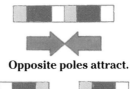

Opposite poles attract.

Matching poles repel.

Pointing north

Did you know that the Earth acts like a giant magnet and attracts other magnets towards its north pole? Try this experiment with two needle-magnets to see how the Earth pulls on magnets.

1 Float a small piece of paper in a bowl of water and rest a needle-magnet on it. When the needle is still, mark which way it points.

First needle points this way.

2 Now do the same with the second needle-magnet. Both needles should point the same direction, which is along a north-south line.

How to find north

To find out which end of your needle-magnet points north, you can either use a compass or you can use your shadow. Go outside at midday on a sunny day. If you are north of the equator, your shadow will point north. If you are south of the equator, it will point south.

Make an electromagnet

If you pass an electric current around a piece of iron, it will turn into a temporary magnet, called an electromagnet. As soon as the current stops flowing, the electromagnet stops working. Here is a way to make your own electromagnet that you can turn on and off.

Never use household electricity for experiments. It is much too strong, and can kill.

You will need
1m (40in) of insulated wire
Large iron nail
Sticky tape
Scissors
1.5 volt battery

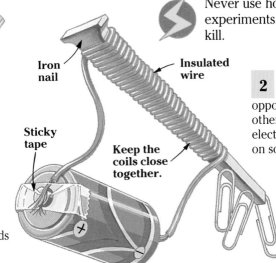

Iron nail

Insulated wire

Sticky tape

Keep the coils close together.

1 Wind the insulated wire tightly around the nail 30 times. Then use scissors to strip about 2cm (0.75in) of plastic covering from both ends of the wire.

2 Tape one end of the wire to the end of the battery marked +. Touch the opposite end of the battery with the other end of the wire. Now your electromagnet should be working. Test it on some paper-clips.

3 Take the wire off the battery. If the nail is made from pure iron, the paper-clips will drop off slowly. (If the nail contains some steel, it becomes a permanent magnet.)

Did you know?

Hovering "maglev" trains, like the Japanese trial model shown here, are operated by powerful electromagnets. Magnets on the base of the train and its track push apart and make the train hover just above the track. Magnets on the sides of the track and the train are controlled automatically, so they pull from the front and push from the rear to drive the train along.

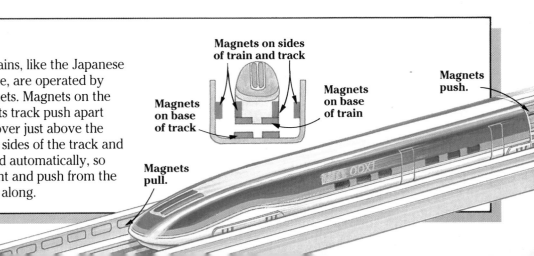

Magnets on sides of train and track

Magnets on base of track

Magnets on base of train

Magnets push.

Magnets pull.

CHARGING UP

Have you made your hair crackle by combing it, or noticed dust clinging to a record? These are effects of electric charge, or static electricity The experiments on these two pages investigate electric charge. They work best on a dry day.

Sticky balloon

Did you know that you can stick a balloon to yourself without glue or sticky tape? It should work best if you are wearing something made of wool. If the balloon doesn't stick very well the first time, try rubbing it on different clothes, or even on your hair.

Blow up a balloon, then rub it vigorously against your sweater or your hair, about ten times. Hold it to your sweater or hair for a moment, and then let go of it. It should stick.

Why the balloon sticks

When the balloon and the sweater rub together, each one gains a different type of electric charge. The balloon becomes negatively charged, and the sweater becomes positively charged. These opposite charges attract each other, like opposite poles of magnets.

More about charge

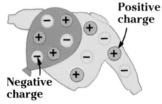

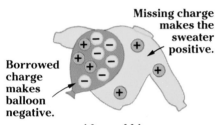

Missing charge makes the sweater positive.

Borrowed charge makes balloon negative.

Positive charge

Negative charge

Before rubbing

After rubbing

The two types of charge are usually balanced: there is the same amount of both charges in everything. The balance in some things can be upset by rubbing them together.

The balloon borrows some of the sweater's negative charge, becoming negatively charged. The sweater becomes positively charged, by losing some of its negative charge.

Pushing apart

This is a trick using two balloons which may surprise your friends. As well as the balloons, you will need nylon thread, sticky tape and something soft and woolly to rub on the balloons.

1 Cut two equal lengths of nylon thread and tape them to the top of a door-frame, spacing them about 2.5cm (1in) apart.

2 Tie one balloon to the end of each thread, so they are hanging at the same height. They should be touching.

3 Now rub the balloons with the woolly thing to charge them, one at a time. Let go of them and see how they hang now.

Door-frame

Sticky tape

Nylon thread

Woolly scarf

Why the balloons push apart

Things which are made of the same material always take the same charge, so both balloons become negatively charged when you rub them. Matching charges of static electricity push each other away, like matching poles of magnets.

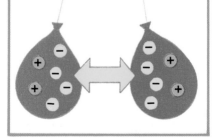

Picking up

Here are some suggestions for experiments that you could try to see how charged things affect uncharged ones. You can make them behave in some quite surprising ways.

Can you make the paper dance?

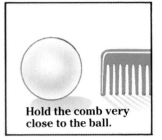

Hold the comb very close to the ball.

Don't let the pen touch the water.

Charge up a plastic pen, then hold it over some small pieces of tissue paper.

Charge a balloon. Then hold it against the wall or the ceiling, and quickly let go of it.

Hold a charged plastic pen or comb near a ping-pong ball. Try to lead it across the table.

Turn on the tap to make a very thin stream of water. Hold a charged pen near the water.

What's happening

Any charged object can temporarily charge something else (as long as that thing can hold a charge), in the same way as a magnet can make temporary magnets out of other metals. This is called induction.

How induction works

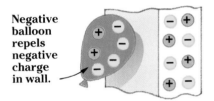

Negative balloon repels negative charge in wall.

When a negatively charged object, like a balloon, meets something uncharged, like a wall, it pushes away the negative charge closest to it, as it would repel a negatively charged object. So the negative charge next to the balloon

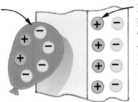

Negative balloon attracts positive part of wall.

Positive part of wall attracts negative balloon.

moves to other parts of the wall. Now the balance of charge is disturbed, and the wall next to the balloon becomes positively charged. Because the charges in the wall and the balloon are now opposite, they attract each other.

Did you know?

The negative charge on a balloon leaks away harmlessly into the air or the ground. When a cloud becomes charged, it is discharged much more dramatically, in lightning.

The charges are separated inside a thunder cloud. The top of the cloud becomes positively charged and the bottom becomes negative. The negative charge at the bottom of the cloud induces a positive charge in the ground underneath.

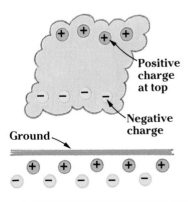

Positive charge at top

Negative charge

Ground

If the charges in the cloud and the ground are great enough, the air cannot stop the cloud discharging to the ground. We see a flash of lightning as the cloud discharges.

BATTERIES AND BUZZERS

The next four pages show you how to make two gadgets and a game using wires, batteries, bulbs and buzzers. You should be able to buy all the things you need in a hardware store. All the experiments use a 4.5 volt battery. The best sort of insulated wire to use for the experiments is single strand bell wire.

 Remember that household electricity is very dangerous, and can kill. Never use it for any experiments.

Burglar alarm

Follow these instructions to make a burglar alarm for your room. When you have wired it up properly, the buzzer will sound every time your door opens.

To make it, you will need a battery, a 6 volt buzzer, insulated wire and aluminium foil, scissors and sticky tape to fix it to the door.

1 Touch the wires on the buzzer to the battery terminals. When it buzzes, firmly tape into place the wire touching the terminal marked +. Leave the other wire on the buzzer loose.

Sticky tape — The buzzer may only work one way around.

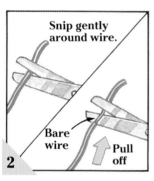

2 Cut two pieces of wire 30cm (12in) long. Strip 2.5cm (1in) of the covering off both ends of each piece, using scissors, as shown above. Be careful not to cut through the wire.

Snip gently around wire. Bare wire. Pull off

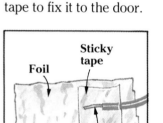

3 Cut two strips of aluminium foil 7.5cm x 2.5cm (3in x 1in). Tape one piece of wire to each of the strips of foil, like this. Make sure that the bare end of the wire is firmly held to the foil.

Foil — Sticky tape — Bare end of wire

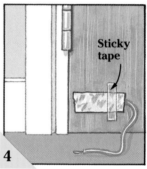

4 Inside the room, tape one strip of foil to the door, near the bottom. Put the sticky tape close to the end where the wire comes out. Smooth the strip of foil flat against the door.

Sticky tape

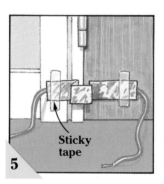

5 Tape the other strip of foil to the door-frame at the same height. Bend this strip so that it sticks out from the wall. A little further along, bend the foil towards the door again.

Sticky tape

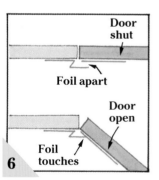

6 Open the door to check that the pieces of foil touch when the door starts to open, and not when you close it again. You may need to bend them more to make sure this happens.

Door shut — Foil apart — Door open — Foil touches

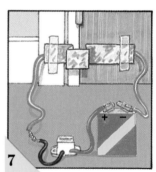

7 Now tape the free end of the wire on the door to the battery terminal marked -. Twist the free end of the wire on the door-frame onto the free wire of the buzzer. Your alarm is ready.

How it works

The buzzer sounds when the door opens because the two pieces of foil act as a switch. When they are apart, the circuit is broken. Because they conduct electricity, the circuit is completed when they touch, and electric current can flow through the buzzer.

Steady hand game

To play this game, you have to guide a wire loop over a bent wire without letting the wires touch. If your hand shakes and the two wires touch, a buzzer sounds. To make the game, start by testing the buzzer and connecting it to the battery as described in step 1 of the burglar alarm.

You will need
6 volt buzzer
4.5 volt battery
Shoe box
1m (40 in) florist's wire
(or other bendy wire
without insulation)
Ball-point pen
50 cm (20 in)
insulated wire
Scissors
Sticky tape

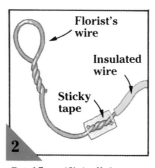

1

With a ball-point pen, make three holes in the lid of the shoe box as shown. Carefully strip 2.5cm (1in) of the covering off each end of the insulated wire.

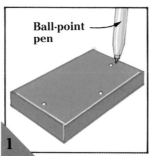

2

Cut 15cm (6in) off the florist's wire and bend one end to make a loop. Twist the other end onto one bare end of the insulated wire, then tape them together.

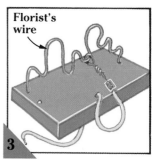

3

Feed the other end of the insulated wire through the middle hole in the lid. Bend the rest of the florist's wire to make a wiggly line. Thread the loop onto it.

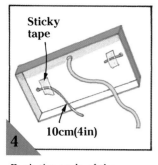

4

Push the ends of the wiggly wire through the holes at the ends of the shoe box lid. Tape both ends to the lid, leaving 10cm (4in) of one end hanging free.

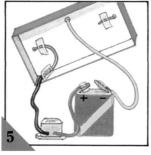

5

Twist together the long end of the wiggly wire and the free buzzer wire. Tape the bare end of the insulated wire to the free battery terminal. The buzzer may sound.

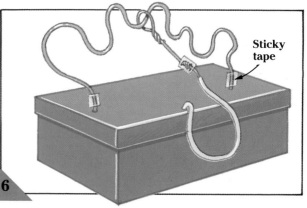

6

Put the battery and buzzer in the box and put on the lid. Wind a little tape around the ends of the wiggly wire. You may need to bend the wire more so it stands up better. Now try the game.

How it works

The wire loop and the wiggly wire act as a switch. When they touch, they complete the circuit, so the buzzer sounds. The tape at the ends of the wiggly wire stops the buzzer sounding when the loop is there, because it insulates the wiggly wire from the loop, so the circuit cannot be completed.

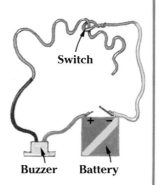

If nothing happens

If the buzzer does not sound when it should, check for a loose connection in your circuit. Are all the correct wires properly twisted together? You could also test your buzzer again, and try another battery, in case yours is running down.

MAKE A DOOR ENTRY SYSTEM

These two pages show you how to make a signal to put outside your door that tells people whether to come in or not. The controls are inside the room, so you can change the lights: green for "come in", and red for "go away".

You will need

Long cardboard tube
2 pieces of cardboard
  12 cm x 20 cm (5 in x 8 in)
1 piece of cardboard
  5 cm x 10 cm (2 in x 4 in)
Aluminium foil
2 4·5 volt torch bulbs
Red and green cellophane
Insulated wire
4·5 volt battery
3 drawing pins
1 paper clip
2 corks, scissors
Glue, sticky tape

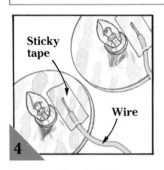

1 7.5cm (3in)

Cut the cardboard tube into two pieces about 7.5cm (3in) long. Cut a small square hole about half-way down each of these short tubes.

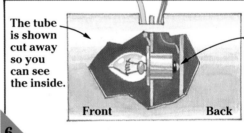

2

Glue foil, shiny side up, to one side of one large piece of cardboard. Cut out four discs of foil-covered cardboard to fit tightly inside the tubes.

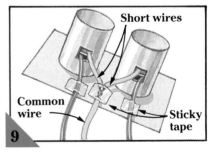

3 Foil · Bulb · Slits

Cut slits in the centre of two discs. Push a bulb into each one, with the glass on the foil side. They must fit snugly. Save the other discs for step 6.

4 Sticky tape · Wire

Cut two pieces of wire 15cm (6in) long and bare the ends.* Tape one bare wire to the foil on each of the two discs with bulbs in them.

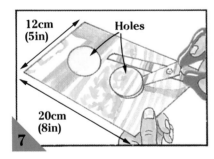

5

Push a bulb disc into each tube and wedge it inside, about half-way down. Feed the wire out of the hole in the side of the tube, as shown.

6 The tube is shown cut away so you can see the inside. · Front · Back · The foil on this disc must be touching the back of the bulb.

Cut three wires long enough to reach loosely from the door to where the switch will be. Bare the ends, and put one wire aside. Tape a long wire to the foil on each of the two discs without bulbs. Carefully push a disc into the back of each tube, feeding the wire through the hole.

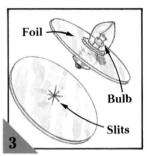

7 12cm (5in) · Holes · 20cm (8in)

Cut two circular holes in the second large piece of cardboard. Cut them one above the other, big enough for the tubes to fit into snugly. This is the panel to hold your lights onto the door-frame.

8

Push the back of each tube a little way into one of the holes, so the tubes are held onto the panel, as shown in the picture. The bulbs and the wires should both be on the same side.

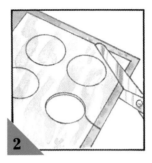

9 Short wires · Common wire · Sticky tape

Twist together one end of the third long wire (the common wire) with the free ends of the two short wires. Tape the common wire and the other two long wires to the panel, to support their weight.

10 Tape the panel firmly to the door-frame outside your room, at the hinged side. Tape a red piece of cellophane over the end of the tube at the top and a green piece over the end of the bottom one.

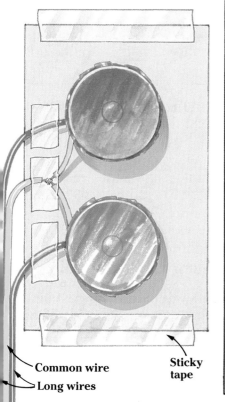

Common wire

Long wires

Sticky tape

Behind the door

11 Feed the three long wires under the door into your room. Close the door and check that it does not trap the wires. Tape the free end of the common wire to one of the terminals on the battery.

12 To make a switch for the system, stick three drawing-pins into the small piece of cardboard. Bend a paper-clip and attach it to one of the pins. Check that the clip can touch the other two pins one at a time.

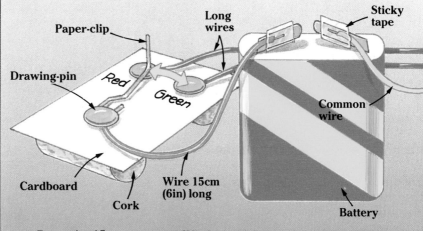

Paper-clip

Drawing-pin

Red

Green

Cardboard

Cork

Wire 15cm (6in) long

Long wires

Sticky tape

Common wire

Battery

13 Cut a wire 15cm (6in) long and bare the ends. Wind one end around the pin holding the paper-clip. Tape its other end to the terminal of the battery which has nothing attached to it.

14 Wind one of the two long wires from the door around each of the other drawing-pins. Stick the ends of all three drawing-pins into corks to stop them from falling out.

15 Now try the switch, and go to the door to see which bulb lights in which position. Label the drawing-pin for the top light RED on the switch, and the bottom light GREEN.

How it works

You have made two circuits which use the same battery, with a switch which can complete only one of the circuits at a time. This means you can switch between red and green, but not have both lights showing at the same time. This type of switch is called a Single Pole Double Throw, or SPDT, switch.

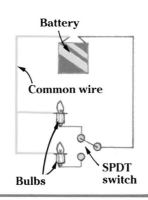

Battery

Common wire

Bulbs

SPDT switch

What the foil does

The foil on the discs makes an electrical connection between the bulbs and the wires, because it conducts electricity. Without the discs, the wires would be hard to connect to the bulbs, and could easily come off. Because it is shiny, the foil also reflects the light from the bulbs, making it brighter.

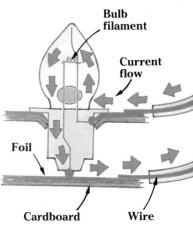

Bulb filament

Current flow

Foil

Cardboard

Wire

SCIENCE INFORMATION

Many of the scientific explanations in this book are simplified. The notes below provide more detailed explanations and supporting information for some of the experiments. You will also find answers to puzzles and a pattern for a propeller.

Pages 6-7, It's a gas

Air contains a mixture of different gases. This chart shows the most important gases in air.

1% Other gases (mainly argon and water vapour).

Around 0.03% Carbon dioxide (CO_2) (the amount of carbon dioxide in the air is variable and rising).

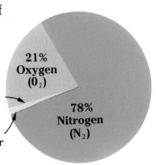

21% Oxygen (O_2)

78% Nitrogen (N_2)

Page 13, Surprising senses

This map of a tongue shows the areas where different tastes are detected most strongly.

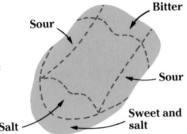

Bitter

Sour

Sour

Sweet and salt

Salt

Page 14, Light and sight

The experiments with shadows on page 14 demonstrate two ways that light can be reflected.

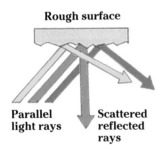

Rough surface

Parallel light rays — Scattered reflected rays

Diffuse reflection

Smooth surface

Parallel light rays — Parallel reflected rays

Regular reflection

"Shadow portrait" shows diffuse reflection. When light rays meet a rough, uneven surface, like a face, some are absorbed and others are reflected in many different directions.

"Spooky shadow" uses regular reflection. When light rays meet the smooth surface of a mirror, they are all reflected in the same direction, making a reflection.

Pages 16-17, Bouncing light

The way that the light beam and its reflection behave in the "Bouncing spotlight" experiment illustrates a law of reflection. This law states that the angle of incidence and the angle of reflection are always the same.

The line at right angles to the mirror at the point where a ray strikes is called the normal. The incoming ray, or

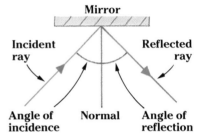

Mirror

Incident ray

Reflected ray

Angle of incidence

Normal

Angle of reflection

incident ray, and the reflected ray are always at the same angle to the normal.

Pages 20-21, Turn and turn again

In the experiment to "Swing the bucket", your arm pulls inwards on the bucket to keep it turning. This inward pull is called the centripetal force. The water pulls outwards in an equal and opposite reaction to the centripetal force, known as the centrifugal effect.

The same force and effect are at work in "Raise the ball" and "Lift the pot".

Page 25, Investigating acids

This chart gives the answers to the acid test.

SUBSTANCES	ACID	NEUTRAL
Apple juice	✓	
Aspirin	✓	
Flour		✓
Lemonade	✓	
Orange squash	✓	
Sugar		✓
Yogurt	✓	
Water		✓*

Water is usually neutral, but added chlorine can make it acidic.

Page 29, Curious colours

The diagram for "How paints mix" shows how the colours of magenta, cyan and yellow mix together. These are the true primary colours for pigments because they mix together equally to make black. The "primary colours" used by artists – red, yellow and blue – are not true primary colours. When you mix them together equally, they make grey, not black.

Pages 40-41, How molecules pull together

All the experiments on pages 40-41 use water, because it is easy to see the effect of the molecules' pull in liquids. Molecules are differently arranged in solids, liquids and gases. This makes the pull, or force, between them different.

Molecules in solids are packed very tightly together in fixed positions. They pull hard on each other, making it difficult for the solid to change shape.

In liquids, the molecules are close to each other and pull towards each other, but they are free to move around and change places, so liquids can change shape.

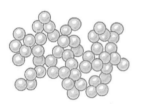

Molecules in gases are very widely spaced, so gases can be squashed. The force holding these molecules together is very weak, so gases are easily dispersed.

Page 42, Frozen solid

"Water level challenge" demonstrates that ice takes up more space than water. This is because the links between ice molecules are longer than the links between water molecules, making them less tightly packed. Most liquids contract when they change into solids because their molecules become more tightly packed.

Page 45, Earth, Sun and Moon

The experiment to "Make an eclipse of the Sun" shows what happens when the Moon passes between the Sun and the Earth, but it is not to scale. The volume of the Sun is more than a million times greater than that of the Earth, and the Sun is over 150 million km (93 million miles) away from the Earth.

To make your experiment to scale, your Sun torch would have to be as big as a hot air balloon and you would need the length of a soccer pitch between it and your model Earth.

Page 48, Warming up

The experiments on page 48 demonstrate that water and air become less dense and expand when they are heated. This is caused by the action of their molecules. The molecules in a substance are constantly moving around and bumping into each other. When a substance is heated up, its molecules move around faster and bump harder against each other. This makes the substance less dense so it take up more space.

Here is a pattern for the "Warm air propeller" Put a piece of thin writing paper over this shape and trace around it.

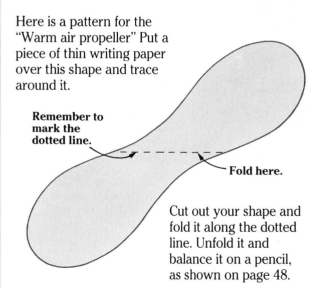

Remember to mark the dotted line.

Fold here.

Cut out your shape and fold it along the dotted line. Unfold it and balance it on a pencil, as shown on page 48.

Page 53, Magnetic attractions

Magnets point to a position in north Canada which is called the magnetic north pole. This is not the same as the geographic north pole. The difference in degrees between magnetic and geographic north varies slightly from country to country. In Britain, magnetic north is 11° west of geographic north.

Pages 54-55, Charging up

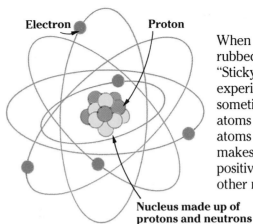

Electron Proton

Nucleus made up of
protons and neutrons

All substances are made up of atoms which contain a lot of charged particles. The positively charged particles are called protons, the negatively charged particles are called electrons. In an uncharged atom, the number of protons is equal to the number of electrons. Electrons are much lighter than protons and are on the edge of atoms so they can move about. The protons are fixed in the centre, or nucleus, of the atom.

When two objects are rubbed together, as in the "Sticky balloon" experiment, electrons sometimes move from the atoms of one object to the atoms of the other. This makes one of the objects positively charged and the other negatively charged.

Pages 56-59, Batteries and buzzers and Make a door entry system

The three circuit diagrams below show how electric current flows between the components in the projects on pages 56-59. The symbols used here can be understood in any country.

Burglar alarm

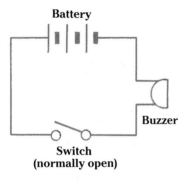

Battery

Buzzer

Switch
(normally open)

Steady hand game

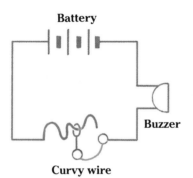

Battery

Buzzer

Curvy wire

Door entry system

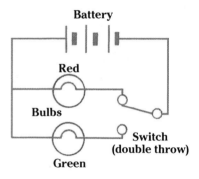

Battery

Red

Bulbs

Switch
(double throw)

Green

Science words

Acid. A chemical that corrodes many metals and reacts with some other chemicals, such as alkalis and carbonates. Acids are detected using indicators.

Alkali. A chemical that takes the acidity away from an acid. Alkalis are detected using indicators.

Atmosphere. The layer of gases and water vapour surrounding the Earth. The main gases in the atmosphere are nitrogen and oxygen.

Carbon dioxide. A colourless gas that is made by adding an acid to a carbonate. Carbon dioxide (CO_2) is found in the atmosphere. It is used by plants to make food and given out by all living things.

Carbonate. A chemical that reacts with an acid to make carbon dioxide gas.

Condensation. The change from a vapour into a liquid. (The opposite of evaporation.)

Density. The amount of mass that a substance has for its size. It is calculated by dividing mass by volume.

Evaporation. The gradual change from a liquid into a vapour. (The opposite of condensation.)

Friction. The force that resists movement when one surface moves over another.

Gravity. The force that pulls objects towards the Earth.

Science words (continued)

Indicator. A substance used to detect acidity and alkalinity. Indicators change colour when they are mixed with acids and alkalis.

Induction. The transfer of the electrical or magnetic state of one object to another.

Inertia. The resistance of an object to any change in motion.

Mass. The amount of matter in a substance, measured in grams (or ounces).

Molecules. The tiny particles of which many substances are made.

Pressure. The force that is exerted over a certain area.

Reaction. The result of two substances mixing with each other. When two substances react together, they change into another substance and may change temperature.

Solution. A liquid containing a dissolved substance. When no more of the substance will dissolve, the solution is saturated.

Water vapour. Molecules of water that are held in the air. Water vapour is made when water evaporates.

INDEX